FORGOTTEN RAILWAYS:

Volume 6

South East England

FORGOTTEN RAILWAYS

Edited by Allan Patmore

Vol

1.	*North East England:*	K. Hoole
2.	*East Midlands:*	P. Howard Anderson
3.	*Chilterns and Cotswolds:*	R. Davies & M. D. Grant
4.	*North and Mid Wales:*	Rex Christiansen
5.	*Scotland:*	John Thomas
6.	*South East England:*	H. P. White
7.	*East Anglia:*	R. S. Joby
8.	*South Wales:*	J. H. R. Page
9.	*North West England:*	John Marshall
10.	*West Midlands:*	Rex Christiansen

Others are in preparation

The master volume, *Forgotten Railways* by H. P. White, in a larger format, has now also been published

Note The description of an old railway route does not imply that there is a public right of way, and readers must obtain permission to enter private land.

Jacket illustration Ramsgate Harbour station in August 1924, which disappeared in the Southern Railway reorganisation of its Thanet lines a year or two later (*Locomotive & General Railway Photographs*)

FORGOTTEN RAILWAYS

Volume 6

South East England

H. P. WHITE

DAVID ST JOHN THOMAS
DAVID & CHARLES

TO JEAN

for being married so long to a railway enthusiast

British Library Cataloguing in Publication Data

White, H. P.

South East England.——2nd rev. ed.——

(Forgotten railways; v. 6)

1. Railroads——England——South East——

Abandonment——History

I. Title II. Series

385'.09422 HE3019.S6

ISBN 0-946537-37-2

First edition published by David & Charles 1976
This second, revised edition published by David St John Thomas and distributed by David & Charles

Set in 11 on 13pt Linotype Baskerville
and printed in Great Britain
by Redwood Burn Ltd Trowbridge Wiltshire
for David St John Thomas
Distributed by David & Charles Publishers plc
Brunel House Newton Abbot Devon

Distributed in the United States of America
by David & Charles Inc
North Pomfret Vermont 05053 USA

Contents

page

BIBLIOGRAPHY AND ACKNOWLEDGEMENTS 6

1 SOUTH EASTERN SCENE 7

2 HAWKHURST AND THE HOPPERS 19
A description of the line – Train services and traffic – Freight traffic – A farewell – The present scene

3 RAILWAYING ON A SHOESTRING 31
Colonel Stephens – The East Kent – The Kent & East Sussex – The West Sussex

4 SECONDARY AND LOCAL LINES ACROSS THE WEALDEN HILLS 49
The defence of Brighton – The passenger-train services – Decline – Description of the lines

5 WEST OF THE BRIGHTON LINE 74
The Mid-Sussex Line – From Shoreham to Horsham – Horsham and Guildford Direct – Rails to Midhurst

6 MINOR HOLIDAY RESORTS 88
Allhallows-on-Sea – The Sheppey Light Railway – Sandgate – Dungeness and New Romney – Crowhurst and Bexhill West – Hayling Island

7 CASUALTIES OF THE FEUD 105
The Feud – The main lines – The Thanet Lines – The Elham Valley – The Feud in the Medway Towns

8 IN SEARCH OF DEEP WATER 122
Tapping the lighter traffic on the Thames – To Gravesend – Port Victoria and Queenborough – Some minor branches – Canterbury and Whitstable – Other port branches

9 A MISCELLANY OF LOST CAUSES 139
The Westerham Valley – To the Devil's Dyke – Kemp Town – The narrow gauge – Stone blocks and iron rails

GAZETTEER 153

INDEX 191

Bibliography and Acknowledgements

As its title implies, this book looks at railways and train services in the South East which because of closures or changed timetable structures are now but memories. It is not a history of the lines concerned although history and social background are an important part of the story. Thus for the history of railways in the area covered by this book I would refer readers to my two books in the *Regional History of the Railways of Great Britain* series, Vol II *Southern England,* and Vol III *Greater London,* and its paperback version *London Railway History,* both of which have full bibliographies and sources.

Since those bibliographies were compiled, Dr. Edwin Course has completed his excellent *Railways of Southern England* (Batsford) in three volumes. The Colonel Stephens railways have been well documented: R. W. Kidner's 'Light Railway Handbooks' series (Oakwood Press 1938) remain an excellent source, and more recent are A. R. Catt *The East Kent Railway* (Oakwood) 1970, S. R. Garrett *The Kent & East Sussex Railway* (Oakwood) 1972 and J. Scott-Morgan *The Colonel Stephens Railways: A Pictorial Survey* (David & Charles, 1978). The *Branch Line Index,* compiled by G. C. Lewthwaite and published by the Branch Line Society (2nd Edition 1971) is an invaluable reference to *The Railway Magazine, Railway World* and *Trains Illustrated.* Mention must be made of R. Crombleholme *The Hawkhurst Railway* (Narrow Gauge and Light Railway Society 1961), D. Gould *The Westerham Valley Railway* (Oakwood 1974) and J. T. Howard Turner *The London, Brighton & South Coast Railway* (3 vols) (Batsford 1977–9).

The author would like to take this opportunity of thanking Mr B. N. Nunns for all his help in providing source material and both him and Mr H. C. L. Tuckett for their assistance with compiling the Gazetteer; Mr. J. Shelton for help in tracing the route of the Croydon, Merstham & Godstone Railway; the late Mr C. F. Klapper for personal details about Colonel H. F. Stephens; Professor J. H. Appleton and Mr J. G. Glover for help on the Peasmarsh–Steyning 'Greenway'; Mr G. D. Whitworth for access to his files of *The Railway Magazine*; Mrs J. Bateson for typing the manuscript; Mr R. Oliver for drawing the text maps; and Dr Edwin Course for help with some dates. Last but by no means least, grateful thanks are due to the Editor of the series, Professor J. A. Patmore for his constant help and encouragement, and to Mrs Jean White who, in the words of the dedication, has been married so long to a railway enthusiast, and understands what this entails.

CHAPTER 1

South Eastern Scene

Throughout the 1950s and 1960s rail closures were news. From the press, radio, and television came a stream of record and comment on individual closure proposals and the consequent protests, inquiries, Ministerial judgement, passenger closure dates and ceremonial last trains. But as each last train completed its journey amid crowds of those who had deserted the line, the closed section ceased to be news as attention switched to the next closure. The subsequent fate of the line, its eventual closure for freight, the lifting of the rails, the withdrawal of the substitute bus service, the way in which those affected found alternative means of transport all went unrecorded by the popular media. The line had become for most a forgotten railway.

Because of the massive and extensive nature of the closures, few have any clear idea of what has resulted from this contraction of the railway system. Not only did the authorities seem anxious to get rid of as much track as possible, they also seemed bent on ridding whole areas of any memories of rail transport.

In many other countries buses often replace some of the less well-patronised trains, and in this way a line can be closed for a part of the day, thus reducing staffing costs. In Great Britain there seems to have been no halfway house of this nature. Elsewhere, if the rails finally disappear, buses and lorries ply in railway liveries; here not only do the closed lines fade into oblivion, but the whole idea of the railway may also become forgotten. 'Forgotten Railways' is a very apt title for the series, of which this book forms a part. Awareness of the full scale of closures is apt to escape all of us. It was a considerable shock to the author when, examining in 1969 a thesis on the development of railways in the East Midlands, he came to realise for the first time how only a few main lines and the odd mineral spur remained of the once extensive rail system serving the 'Grassy Shires'.

But travelling through the countryside with our eyes open we can see frequent traces of forgotten railways. For the practised eye, there are the narrowly parallel lines of overgrown hedges between which trains once ran, but where saplings and brambles are rapidly taking over. There too are the road overbridges with nothing under them, embankments cut away on either side of a road where an underbridge has been removed, 'Railway Inns' with no railway, and 'Station Roads' which no longer lead to a station.

In South East England, however, closures have affected the railway system far less than in most parts of the country. The mileage of forgotten railways, though large, is small in relation to that of lines still open. Even today nowhere is more than ten miles and very few places more than five miles from a railway station which is still open for passenger traffic, and still has a good service. No extensive areas have been completely denuded of their railways; many of the forgotten lines had been forgotten long before 1962, while some lines have even had passenger services restored.

The area covered by this volume lies south of the Thames and east of a line drawn from London's Victoria through Clapham Junction, Wimbledon, Sutton, Epsom, Dorking and Guildford and thence along the Portsmouth Direct railway through Petersfield to Havant. It is largely the area served by three of the pre-Grouping railway companies, the London, Brighton & South Coast, the South Eastern, and the London, Chatham & Dover. For convenience, however, the coincidence is not exact along the western boundary.

In 1923 these three companies handed over a total of 1,095 route miles to the new Southern Railway. Within the area were also 34½ route miles still operated by four independent companies. Any lines which eventually came under the control of London Transport are not included.

In the period 1923 to 1985 9.88 route miles of new line were opened by the Southern Railway, passenger services restored over a further 3½ miles, and 262 route miles were completely closed by the SR and BR. Why was this mileage of closures so small compared with that of other areas? In essence the answer lies in the different roles that railways play in the South East to those elsewhere. These roles have of course changed, as they have everywhere, but although the system has been greatly modified to accommodate changing circumstances, the adaptation has tended to be positive, rather than simply bringing to an end any contribution by the railways to changed transport needs.

At Grouping the functions of the railways in the South East could be summarised for passenger traffic as short-distance inter-urban (87 miles from Victoria to Portsmouth Harbour was the longest run), local traffic in rural areas, suburban and commuter traffic in the London area, holiday traffic to the coastal resorts, and Continental traffic. Unlike the railways to the north of London, passengers accounted for a major part of the revenue. The majority of freight, especially coal, originated outside the area, while much general freight was loaded at the London freight terminals. Apart from Lower Thamesside between Deptford and the Medway Towns, there was little originating industrial traffic. There was also a considerable volume of agricultural traffic and some coal from East Kent.

The half-century after 1923 saw fundamental changes sweep over South East England: the suburban explosion of the inter-war years, the post-war growth of population in the Outer Metropolitan Area (ie beyond the built-up area of Greater London), and rapid industrialisation. Greater London spread far into the countryside of North West Kent and almost obliterated that of Surrey. In the Outer Metropolitan Area growth tended to be aligned in corridors along the main roads and railways along the south bank of the Thames

Estuary, down to Brighton and along the length of the Sussex coast. Between these corridors, wedges of countryside experienced fewer outward changes. There were also the general fundamental changes in the transport scene. Between 1923 and 1950 there was a tremendous growth in bus traffic and in road haulage. Since then road haulage has continued its expansion, car ownership became more nearly universal, and bus traffic declined severely.

All this had tremendous consequences on the railway system of the South East. The most spectacular change was the growth in commuter traffic, a story previously chronicled in the author's *Southern England* and *Greater London* (Vols II and III in the Regional Railway History Series). Suffice here to say that it grew particularly over middle and long distances. In the inner areas of London there was a decline, due first to tram and then to bus competition. Until the middle 1950s where commuter traffic grew there was also a tendency for off-peak traffic to increase, encouraged by frequent services and low fares, but thereafter off-peak bookings tended to fall with increased car ownership. Along the main lines fast and frequent services supported by the commuter traffic kept inter-urban passenger traffic at a higher level than generally experienced elsewhere, in spite of parallel bus services and high levels of car ownership. While the growth of the private car cut into seasonal holiday traffic, day excursion traffic remained at a consistently high level. There were changes in the make-up of continental traffic. First-class passengers declined due to air competition, but 'classic' boat train traffic slowly increased, though not to the same extent as that of accompanied cars. On the other hand, as everywhere else, short-distance rural traffic declined catastrophically, suffering first from bus and then from car competition. Lines without heavy commuter or inter-urban traffic were forced to close. There were only twenty-three season ticket holders from stations on the 'Cuckoo' line when services ceased (p 64).

Freight traffic has also changed. It declined in volume during the inter-war years in the face of road haulage. Agricultural traffic almost disappeared. After the war general freight continued its decline, while coal was also reduced in volume from the mid-1950s onwards. Decline was accelerated in the 1960s due to the transfer of 'sundries' to National Carriers Ltd, the Beeching policy of shedding wagon-load traffic, and the wholesale closure of freight depots. But industrialisation led to a growth in train-load traffic such as cement, petroleum, aggregates and cars, while continental traffic through Dover also increased. On the Southern Region freight traffic during the 1960s was increasing at about the same rate as it was declining over BR as a whole. In the period 1963–74 originating freight traffic on the Southern Region increased by 68 per cent. Now traffic moves in train-loads to and from a very small number of terminals, and for the most part the trains are operated over the main lines. With few exceptions, there is now no freight on the secondary and branch lines, which must justify their existence solely by their passenger traffic. Loss of freight followed by withdrawal of freight facilities has been a factor in line closures here as elsewhere.

The evolution of the railway network

Before reviewing the forgotten lines of South East England, it will be useful to trace briefly the evolution of the railway network, for there are certain basic themes against which the more local factors influencing the promotion, building, operation and closure of the individual lines can be seen in regional perspective.

The physiography of South East England can be likened to the bone structure beneath the face of the region, which is the man-made rural and urban landscapes. Our area stretches between Thames and Channel and is bounded to the west by the great plateau of the chalk downlands of Hampshire.

The central core, the High Weald, is surrounded by a number of horseshoe-shaped rings of varied geology and therefore of great physiographic variety. The open end of the horseshoe lies along the Channel coast north-eastward from

Beachy Head. Wrapped around the High Weald is the low-lying vale of the Weald Clay, its coastal extremities being Pevensey Levels and Romney Marsh respectively. The next horseshoe is the ridge of the Lower Greensand. In Kent this is continuous, presenting a marked scarp to the south and with few gaps through it; at the western end it is a wide band of high, broken, forested country, rising to 965ft at Leith Hill and 918ft at Hindhead. In Sussex it is much less conspicuous as far as Pulborough and insignificant eastward thereof.

This horseshoe is separated by a narrow clay vale from the ring of chalk downland with its high and continuous in-facing scarp. The North Downs exceed 700ft and the South Downs 800ft. Both provide a formidable barrier, passable by means of a number of low-level gaps. The North Downs slope gently northwards to the plain bordering the Thames. Similarly the South Downs slope to the Sussex Coastal Plain, which gradually widens westward from Brighton.

Throughout history the region has been dominated socially and economically by London, and the main routes have always fanned out from the capital to terminal points along the coast. All must cross the high ground of Downs and Weald. Even the route along the south of the Thames Estuary must strike inland from Faversham and cross the wind-swept Downs of East Kent before Dover is reached.

The first main line, opened in 1841, strode straight southward across the grain of the country from London Bridge to Brighton. The route involved massive earthworks and considerable tunnelling. From this trunk the South Eastern line to Dover branched off at Redhill and ran the length of the Weald Clay Vale of Kent to Ashford, thence to Dover by the spectacular coastal section from Folkestone. The route was completed in 1844.

Perhaps the overriding reason for the South Eastern's victory over rival schemes was the possibility of branch lines, and by 1851 most important Kentish towns had been reached. From Tonbridge the main line through Tunbridge Wells to Hastings was completed in 1851. Maidstone was reached in

1844 by a branch from Paddock Wood. A long and important branch led north eastward down the Stour Valley from Ashford to Canterbury, Ramsgate and Margate (1846) and from this line there was a branch from Minster to Deal (1847). The Medway Towns however, were reached by the North Kent line opened in 1849.

The North Kent was owned by the SER. An independent company, the East Kent was floated to continue this, the 'natural' route to Canterbury and Dover, originally followed by the Roman Watling Street. Owing to a misjudgement on the part of the SER, the East Kent became part of a rival route to Dover owned by the LCDR. Opened throughout in 1861, it ran from Victoria through Bromley, Chatham, Faversham and Canterbury. Its completion sparked off thirty years of bitter rivalry between the two companies, made worse by the clash of personalities between Sir Edward Watkin, Chairman of the SER, and James Staats Forbes, who directed the fortunes of the LCDR. In consequence rival lines were built to virtually all the Kentish towns. The LCDR reached Margate and Ramsgate by a line from Faversham completed in 1861. In a piecemeal fashion it also provided a third route to Dover by the line from Swanley Junction to Ashford (1884) through Maidstone. The riposte of the SER included the Sevenoaks Cut-off from St Johns on the North Kent to Tonbridge on the original SER line (1868). Both companies also opened numerous branch lines in the London suburbs and the open country of North West Kent.

The generalisation is often made that redundant and unnecessary lines were widely built by rival companies. If ever there was promotion of apparently redundant lines it was as a result of the 'feud' between the SER and the LCDR which was only brought to an end with the fusion in 1899 of the two companies into the South Eastern & Chatham Railways Managing Committee. But such has been the growth in the economy and the population of Kent that none of the main lines and few of the branches have in fact become redundant. In this respect Kent is in complete contrast with the West

Riding, where the Great Northern built a complete system alongside the original created by the Lancashire & Yorkshire, Midland, and London & North Western Railways. In spite of the much greater degree of industrialisation, the loss of freight and passenger traffic has been so great that the GNR lines have almost all been abandoned.

The LBSCR extended its system by two very important lines from Brighton. The 'East Coast line' (now 'Coastway East') ran eastward serving Lewes, Eastbourne and Hastings, which was reached in 1851, while the 'West Coast line' ('Coastway West') ran westward through Worthing and Chichester to Portsmouth, being completed throughout in 1847. The principal main lines of the company were completed by the Mid-Sussex line through Dorking and Horsham to join the West Coast line at Arundel Junction.

Like the other two companies the LBSCR fostered an extensive and complex suburban system to the south of London. It is not the place here to describe the Southern Region's suburban system, inherited from the three companies. It is however important to remember that each company developed two London terminals, one for the City and one in the West End. The LBSCR owned part of London Bridge (City) and part of Victoria (West End), the SER part of London Bridge, Cannon Street (City) and Charing Cross (West End), and the LCDR part of Victoria and its City complex of the three adjacent stations of Blackfriars, Ludgate Hill and Holborn Viaduct. The complexity of the suburban system is explicable in terms of each of three companies having both a City and a West End focus. Add in the LSWR, and the Southern Region inherited seven of the fifteen London termini. Equally significant is the fact that in 1960, of the 626,000 passengers arriving daily at these fifteen termini, 419,000 (67 per cent) arrived at the seven SR termini and 207,000 (33 per cent) at the other eight.

The vast increase in traffic coming on to the railways of South East England could be accommodated only by drastic improvements in their technical equipment. The principal one has been electrification, a story traced in *Southern England*. Sufficient to say that the SR suburban system was electrified for the greater part in the years between 1909 and 1930, though most lines were converted after 1923. In that year the new Southern Railway had taken over eighty-three route miles of electrified line, while in the five years to 1928 a further 193½ route miles were converted. Thereafter the SR concentrated on main line electrification. Between the conversion of the line to Brighton in 1933 and the SER line to Dover and Ramsgate in 1962 all the main lines in our area were electrified, save that between Tonbridge and Hastings, which was converted in 1986. Many branch lines were also converted. There is little doubt this extensive electrification was another factor behind the small mileage of closures. It must be more than a coincidence that the post-Beeching closures were, with one minor exception, of the non-electrified lines, especially when it is realised that some of the closed lines carried more passengers than some of the electric lines remaining open.

The plan of the book

The network of main lines, always a close-meshed one, has survived almost intact for the reasons just outlined. Even branch lines have survived to a surprising extent, if judged by national standards. It is therefore not really feasible to treat the forgotten railways of South East England area by area, for the closed lines are isolated and scattered. Instead they have been grouped by connecting themes.

Thus the theme of lines built to serve minor and often unsuccessful holiday resorts links together a number of short and scattered branch lines (Chapter 6), while similarly another group of forgotten lines can be identified as those built to service minor ports (Chapter 8). Another linking theme is that of Colonel Stephens' group of independent lines (Chapter 3), which were linked by common ownership, though widely scattered geographically. Consideration of the Hawkhurst branch (Chapter 2) provides an opportunity to recall a forgotten traffic, once very important on lines that remain open, the annual flood of hop-pickers from the London slums to the Kentish hop gardens. On the other hand, the closed lines of the Central Weald do form a sufficiently compact group to be dealt with on a geographical basis, as is done in Chapter 4.

Another advantage of this approach is that attention can be given to forgotten sources of traffic. The unique annual exodus of hop-pickers from the London slums to the Kentish hop-gardens is now a fading memory. The opportunity has therefore been taken to describe this traffic as a whole, including that passing over lines still open, rather than merely in connection with the defunct Hawkhurst branch (Chapter 2). Occasionally however a linking theme and a geographical area do coincide. Thus closed lines in the central Weald (Chapters 4 and 5) have a common functional history within a compact geographical area.

Each chapter will deal with a selected theme and is intended to serve as an introduction to the forgotten railways linked with that theme. In the case of each line an attempt will be made to give the general reader an overall picture of the events leading up to its opening, its traffic and train service, and its eventual decline and closure, together with some idea of the relationship between the line and the countryside through which it passed.

The Gazetteer is intended to provide detailed information of what there is to see on the ground, and is primarily for the use of the person who wishes to visit a particular line. It has been prepared with the following purposes in mind:

1. To summarise the basic information about each line mentioned in the text, including opening and closure dates.
2. To list in detail the physical remains of each line.
3. To describe the scenic background of the lines and to mention the possibilities for visiting them.

Then and now on the Hawkhurst Branch – I
1. A pull-and-push train, propelled from Hawkhurst, passes Churn Lane Siding on its way to Paddock Wood in 1956.
2. The same location in 1974; the gate-post on the extreme right of the upper picture still survives.

Then and now on the Hawkhurst Branch – II
3. The last up train of the day, the 20.06 collects vans of pot-plants at Hawkhurst in 1961.
4. The site of Hawkhurst station in 1974, looking towards Paddock Wood, with the goods shed on the right and locomotive shed on left.

CHAPTER 2

Hawkhurst and the Hoppers

Between Tonbridge and Ashford the main line of the South Eastern Railway from London Bridge to Dover, opened in stages between 1842 and 1844, runs the length of the Vale of Kent for 26½ miles, in virtually a dead straight and only slightly undulating line. In steam days it was the aim of some drivers to cover the distance in even time start-to-stop. Today, a semi-fast electric multiple unit leaves Tonbridge every hour and, after the Paddock Wood stop, is timed to cover the 21¼ miles on to Ashford in twenty-two minutes.

To the north the Vale is bounded by the steep and continuous scarp of what is known to geologists as the Lower Greensand Cuesta, and to most local inhabitants as the Ragstone Ridge. To the south the land rises much more gradually to the High Weald. The last named, with its parallel ridges separated by deep valleys, is not easy country for railway building. Also, in the mid-nineteenth century the area within the angle formed by the Tonbridge–Ashford and Tonbridge–Hastings lines lacked economic attraction for railway promoters. It was very well wooded and in the open spaces were scattered small and rather poor mixed farms, each with its small hop-garden. There were only three small towns or large villages, Cranbrook with a completely decayed cloth industry, Hawkhurst and, further east, Tenterden.

Although it is not the sort of country to invite railway speculators, a number of schemes were put forward, but all failed to make headway. Local enthusiasm was not matched by local capital and outside support was not forthcoming; there were no large landowners in the Kentish High Weald and no wealthy industrialists. The South Eastern was never very interested in promoting local lines, unless the objective was to serve somewhere of the importance of Maidstone, reached in 1844 by a branch from Paddock Wood. The company preferred to wait for a branch to be built with local capital and then to purchase it at a knock-down price when traffic failed to come up to expectations. Thus branches southward from the main line were promoted at intervals, but failed to make headway. In 1844 the Headcorn & Rye, in 1845 the Rye Harbour Direct (this time at least with nominal South Eastern support) from Paddock Wood, and in 1857 a Marden and Cranbrook branch all failed to reach Parliament, or even if they did, the Statute Book.

In 1864, however, the South Eastern's interest was aroused by the threat to its Mid-Kent monopoly by the London, Chatham & Dover, working through the nominally-independent Sevenoaks, Maidstone & Tonbridge Company. It seemed to the SER that Tonbridge would certainly not be the south-eastern limit of its rival's ambition. By 1866 the SER had lost interest following the financial collapse of the Chatham, and even felt able to oppose a scheme for a Weald of Kent Railway from Paddock Wood to Hythe via Cranbrook and Tenterden. Nothing further happened for a decade. Then the Cranbrook & Paddock Wood Company was floated, and on 8 August 1877 obtained its Act of Incorporation. The promoters were local men with limited capital. They had chosen for the *motif* of their seal a hop leaf, significant in the economy of the area and in the history of the Hawkhurst branch.

Hops are a traditional crop in Mid-Kent. In the fourteenth century the then Vicar of Goudhurst, entitled to the tithes from gardens, tried to obtain legal sanction for considering hops as a garden crop, for as a field crop the tithes were rectorial and went to his monastic masters. He failed, but ever since Kentish hop-fields have been 'gardens'. With the nineteenth century growth of the industrial population, consumption of beer increased and large-scale brewing developed;

the demand for hops increased and during the latter part of the century the primitive gardens gave place to more modern ones concentrated on large farms. Paddock Wood became the principal centre of hop cultivation in Mid-Kent, the hop-gardens spreading over a large area, served by the Maidstone West branch as far as Wateringbury, by the main line as far as Pluckley, and by the Hawkhurst branch.

Development of the hop industry depended on the railway for two reasons. Moving the crop to market in the 2cwt sacks, invariably known as 'pockets', required heavy transport, while the hand-picking of the hops from the 'bines' needed large amounts of casual labour for about three weeks in September. With the growth of the industry local supplies of labour became inadequate, but the railway allowed a vast labour reservoir to be tapped—the slums of south-east London.

Thus came about the annual invasion of Mid-Kent by thousands of poorer working-class families. Men, women and children picked hops by day, slept in lines of 'hopper-huts', and made merry in the evenings and at week-ends in and around the local pubs. For them it was their annual holiday, their only spell of country air and green fields. One woman wrote to a farmer: 'I have come hopping with you for the last twenty years and would like to come again this year. As you well know, I have just had my tenth child—the Headcorn air agrees with me'!

But to return to the Hawkhurst story. Work was started on the branch in 1879, but funds were lacking and the SER remained deaf to pleas for help, bringing construction to a halt. Even so, the promoters obtained a second Act on 12 July 1882 authorising a $1\frac{1}{2}$ mile extension to Hawkhurst. It was then clear nothing would be done until the SER took over, which it did later that year. Work began again in 1891. The ceremonial first train, drawn by a Cudworth E class 2–4–0 wreathed in bunting, steamed in to Goudhurst (then called Hope Mill for Goudhurst and Lamberhurst) on 1 October 1892. Public traffic began the same day. The line on to Hawkhurst opened to all traffic on 4 September 1893.

A description of the line

The line's Engineer was none other than Colonel H. F. Stephens. Though the line was always operated as an orthodox branch and never formed part of his ramshackle shoestring empire (Chapter 3), it always had something of the Stephens stamp. It was a largely surface line and overcame the considerable obstacles of the High Weald by heavy gradients, sharp curves, and the minimum of earthworks. The station buildings had corrugated iron walls and elliptical roofs over wooden frames.

The line was characterised by its gradients and by the inconvenient placing of the stations. Only Horsmonden was near to its village. Goudhurst was a mile from the village and 250ft below, Cranbrook all but two miles from the centre of the little town, and Hawkhurst nearly 1¼ miles out from the village along a very hilly road. But the hilly fertile countryside with its orchards, hop-gardens and timbered farmhouses made it one of the most picturesque branch lines in the country.

Paddock Wood was (and still is to a great extent) a typical SER station. The two through platforms were served by loops off the main lines, so that fast trains could overtake stopping ones. At the country end of each platform was a short bay, that on the down side being used by the Maidstone trains and that on the up side by those to Hawkhurst. All the scheduled branch trains started from here, though for many years the last up train ran through to Tonbridge, because of the through vans it carried and because the engine was serviced at Tonbridge shed. The main building at Paddock Wood was on the down platform, a large two-storey Italianate building which remained unaltered until pulled down about 1968. At the time of the opening in 1842 there was not even a farmhouse nearby, and the station was named after a small wood cut down for its construction. The post-railway settlement (of 4,805 souls in 1971) grew up on the south side of the line and a low range of offices was erected on the up side about 1895. The goods yard was on the up side, though the original goods shed was on the down side at the London end of the station. Beyond the station at the country end was the small Keylands marshalling yard from which the Hawkhurst freight trains started. The large depot for fruit and vegetables railed from the Continent, opened in 1974, occupies the site of Keylands Yard.

The Hawkhurst branch passed under the signal box which was built high up on girders. It then ran parallel to the main line for seven tenths of a mile before gradually diverging from it. On a number of occasions when the author was travelling on the last down branch train of the day, the Hawkhurst and main line trains started simultaneously and made a race of it, the two-coach pull-and-push with its H class 0–4–4T often beating the three-coach Ashford train hauled by an E1 4–4–0, or a 2–6–0.

The branch ran on the level for a further mile to Churn Lane crossing. Here there was a siding, unused for public traffic at least since 1940, but which latterly saw occasional use to stable empty wagons. Just beyond was an accommodation crossing on a drive to a large farm. In 1938 the branch freight would pause here for hop-pockets to be loaded straight into a box wagon.

The gradients now quickly steepened to 1 in 66. The H class tanks would blast their slow way between the orchards, but the heavier 'hopper' specials sometimes could not make it. On 29 September 1951 the stock for the 13.15 'Hop-pickers' Return Special' from Hawkhurst was being worked up from Paddock Wood by a D class 4–4–0 31729 tender-first, which slipped to a stand just short of the 86yd tunnel at Horsmonden. The sanding gear could not be used when working in reverse so a re-start was impossible. The fireman walked on to the station to telephone for assistance. Help came in the shape of C class 0–6–0 31717 from Tonbridge, which assisted in the rear to Horsmonden, where it ran round and piloted for the rest of the journey.

Horsmonden (four miles) had a passing loop, but only a

single platform behind which on the up side was the small goods yard. The loop adjoined a fruit-packing station, which loaded and despatched the occasional wagon.

Beyond the station the single line ran up the valley of the Teise to Goudhurst Station (6½ miles). Here were two platforms and in later years the first up and down passenger trains of the day crossed. On the up platform was the usual tin shed, next to it a three-storey brick stationmaster's house. The two-road goods yard lay behind. Goudhurst starred as the station in a children's television serial screened in the mid-1950s called *The Old Pull-and-Push.*

The line crossed the main road on the level and climbed on up the valley circling the hill-top village. After a mile Pattenden siding was passed, no further from the village than was the station. The occasional wagon of shoddy (cotton waste), used to manure the hops, was off-loaded here up to the end of the line's existence. The gradients steepened and the line wound up through woodland to Cranbrook (ten miles). Like Horsmonden there was a loop, but only a single platform. This was on the down side and had the standard station building and a large stationmaster's house. There was also a large goods yard.

Climbing was resumed at 1 in 85 up to the 178yd Badger's Oak tunnel, the summit of the line. With steam shut off, the locomotive coasted down the short length of 1 in 85 to Hawkhurst (11½ miles). Hawhurst was laid out as a through station in case the line should be extended to Rye. There was a loop with such a short head-shunt that in the hop season a pull-off locomotive was provided. The short platform with its corrugated-iron office building was on the down side, and behind them a four-road goods yard equipped with a large goods shed and facilities for discharging petrol wagons, the latter being out of use for many years before closure. The two-road locomotive shed, in good order though disused since 1931, together with the signal box was on the up side.

Train services and traffic

The passenger service varied little over the years. The inaugural frequency of ten trains daily each way (two on Sundays) was unchanged in the 1906 timetable. In 1912 the branch train would have been made up of elderly six-wheelers hauled by a Q class 0–4–4T. World War I saw cuts in the service and the Sunday trains disappeared for ever. In 1925 the frequency was eight each way, but the trains would have been of bogie stock. Former LCDR class R1 0–4–4T locomotives had been equipped with pull-and-push control gear, and allocated to Hawkhurst. By 1930 there was an extra Saturday service, but the next year the first up and last down services had been taken off with the closing of the locomotive shed and the stabling of all locomotives at Tonbridge. In 1934 an unbalanced early up working from Hawkhurst was introduced, and by 1938 the timetable had taken on its final form with seven up and six down trains with an extra working on Saturday afternoon.

In 1951 the first up train left at 07.32. The stock, a two-coach pull-and-push set of ex-LSWR coaches, was kept at Hawkhurst overnight. The locomotive, usually a C class 0–6–0, came down with the 04.50 freight from Paddock Wood. The train would arrive at Paddock Wood with a handful of commuters for Tonbridge and London and about 120 school children en route for Tonbridge. By 1956 the train was strengthened with a non-corridor second, the three coaches coming back on the mid-day freight.

The other six trips were made by another pull-and-push set hauled by an H class 0–4–4T (the last R1 was withdrawn from Tonbridge in 1956), the locomotive invariably leading from Paddock Wood. By a special regulation, guards were not carried on the pull-and-push workings, except the first up train. School children crowded the 16.25 from Paddock Wood, but otherwise few trains carried more than a dozen passengers, and the author was often the only passenger on the 19.28 by the time it reached Hawkhurst. In 1958 the

Kent Education Committee contracted with Maidstone & District Motor Services to provide special buses for the scholars, and the branch lost the mainstay of its passenger service.

The writing was on the wall and early closure was heralded by an outburst of station-painting and the suspension of economy measures in signalling! There was no doubt that the line was overstaffed. It was controlled, uniquely on the Southern, by Tyer's tablet, and each station had a signal box manned on two shifts. There was also a booking porter on each shift and, until a few years before closure, each station had a stationmaster as well. But the most stringent of economies would not have been enough; there was just not the traffic potential, and even then it was far more convenient to drive to Etchingham or Staplehurst with their very adequate service to London. Closure on 12 June 1961 was like the death of a very dear but elderly friend, sad but inevitable.

The special traffic on the Hawkhurst branch had great interest. The chief of these were the 'Hopper' specials. The hop-picking season started early in September and lasted for about three weeks. The specials almost invariably originated at London Bridge Low Level and called at New Cross or New Cross Gate. To these three stations thousands of families would make their way, wheeling infants and mountains of impedimenta in old prams. They brought with them 'advice cards' from the farmer for whom they were going to work, giving the date he wanted them to begin. The cards authorised them to buy cheap rate tickets.

The most elderly stock was used though the last six-wheeled sets were withdrawn by 1935. Thereafter former SECR 'long sets' were used, They were usually of non-corridor stock with the characteristic 'birdcage' lookouts on the brake vans at the ends. Normally the trains were of eight or nine coaches, but were at times reduced to six, with up to four utility vans added for the baggage.

The specials converged by every possible route on Paddock

Wood, where a temporary train control office was set up. Not only was the main line through Orpington used, but routes via Swanley and Sevenoaks, Oxted and Edenbridge, and even the Dartford Loop and Strood. From Paddock Wood they went on to Hawkhurst, Pluckley and the Maidstone West branch. Three weeks later the return specials would have to be organised, while at week-ends special trains for 'Hop-pickers' friends' would also be provided and worked in with the end-of-season holiday traffic.

On Saturday 21 September 1946, the Special Traffic Notice showed sixteen specials and two further conditional ones leaving London Bridge between 08.33 and 16.18, eight for Maidstone West, eight for Pluckley and two for Paddock Wood, carrying train numbers from H61 to H79. Eight ran via Orpington, five via East Croydon and Oxted, two via the Mid-Kent and Oxted, one via Swanley, one via Woolwich and Strood and the other via the Dartford Loop. Extra connecting trains were provided for Hawkhurst and Pluckley. On Sundays there would be anything up to six return trains leaving Hawkhurst.

Although in 1952 4,442 pickers and 23,000 friends travelled in fifty-six special trains, this traffic was already in decline. With rising living standards and paid holidays, fewer hoppers came down each year and more and more of those who still came travelled in cars and vans. Faced with a declining labour force, the farmers bought mechanical pickers, accelerating the decline. By 1959 only a single two-coach train came down the Hawkhurst branch on Sundays, with a return through working to London Bridge in the evening. During the week the normal service was adequate. By the time the Hawkhurst branch had closed and the other lines had been electrified the hopping traffic was a memory.

The other principal sources of special traffic were the boarding schools of the area. Benenden sported a special train to and from Charing Cross, usually six corridor coaches hauled by an E1 or D1 4-4-0. Cranbrook was the station for Benenden, but as with all specials the train went on to

Hawkhurst for the locomotive to run round. The boys of Cranbrook school had to be content with service trains, strengthened to four coaches. Trunks and other end-of-term bric-a-brac reached such proportions that several utility vans were needed. These were loaded at Hawkhurst and Cranbrook, attached to the daily up goods and forwarded from Paddock Wood by parcels train.

Freight traffic

Freight traffic on the Hawkhurst branch was the usual type on this sort of line; coal, fertilisers and feeding stuffs together with groceries inwards: grain, fruit and hops outwards. In 1937 the working timetable showed two down freights from Paddock Wood and another conditional working for Goudhurst. In the up direction there were two conditional trains and a further one from Goudhurst. All these were 'market' trains and carried wagons for Blackfriars Goods attached to partially-fitted freights at Paddock Wood.

After the war the freight traffic fell off drastically. Hops were conveyed by road to Paddock Wood, while the market produce went by road all the way to London. By 1952 there were two freights down the branch from Paddock Wood, the early service was worked by the locomotive returning with the first up passenger train, and a round trip leaving Paddock Wood in the late afternoon. In 1956 the sundries traffic was concentrated on Etchingham, the locomotive for the first passenger train coming down light. A diesel shunter made a round trip from Paddock Wood at mid-day. There was now little traffic other than coal, and after closure this was delivered to the merchants from a railhead at Staplehurst.

In the last years of the branch, a very important traffic was in pot-plants from local nurseries for F. W. Woolworth & Co Ltd. Carriage charges would normally have been in the region of £1,000 a week. The plants were loaded at Hawkhurst into passenger vans and hauled behind the locomotive which propelled the last up train. This ran through to Tonbridge for the transfer of the vans. In the week before Mothering Sunday a special parcels train was run. Further wagons might be added at Horsmonden from the fruit-packing station and the pull-and-push would arrive at Tonbridge towing more vans behind the locomotive than coaches were being propelled by it.

A Farewell

Throughout the 1950s, the author frequently used the branch in a variety of circumstances. For him the spirit of the Hawkhurst branch was epitomised by journeys from London through many a summer evening after a long day's work. One of the reasons for the unpopularity of the branch for commuters was the lack of a connection off the 17.40 from Cannon Street. If the 16.32 was too early, one had to await the 18.18 to Ramsgate, preferably in the buffet. The Ramsgate was invariably hauled by a Bulleid Pacific and there were no spare seats in its eleven coaches. At Tonbridge the last three coaches were detached and the front part of the train left for Ashford with about a hundred passengers. A 4–4–0 would back onto the Bulleid three-coach set to take it on all-stations to Ashford. At Paddock Wood a dozen or so passengers crossed over the footbridge for the Hawkhurst train waiting in its bay, while as many again changed into the Maidstone train. The Hawkhurst and Ashford trains would often blast out together, and the former would begin its half-hour journey through the ripening orchards, pausing at each station to set down two or three passengers. At 19.58 Hawkhurst was reached, on a ridge-top high above the surrounding country. A short walk home followed along a quiet country road, the only sound coming from the H tank picking up the flower vans. It was not just forty-six miles from Cannon Street, it was a whole world away, while the 100 minute journey encompassed the whole range of operating conditions from main line to country branch, from the busy eight platforms of Cannon Street to the quiet single one of Hawkhurst.

The present scene

The years since 1961 have dealt hardly with the Hawkhurst branch. The region is very intensively cultivated and land values are very high indeed. Gradually the right-of-way has been taken into cultivation, embankments have been bulldozed, cuttings filled and boundary hedges and fences removed so the line can be taken into the orchards, hop-gardens and fields of soft fruit. In many places the former branch has indeed become a forgotten railway and even an eye trained to spot railway remains and aided by a large-scale map has great difficulty in tracing the route, which is now impossible to walk for any distance. A great opportunity has been missed in not preserving the integrity of the right-of-way as a pedestrian or bridle way through the lovely countryside.

Goudhurst station, yard and level crossing has completely disappeared under road widening and expensive houses. Even a short stretch of characteristic green-painted iron fencing remaining in 1974 has since disappeared. The other stations have been put to various uses; Horsmonden is a garage, Cranbrook has been a pottery and Hawkhurst is a wood-turning workshop. The firm uses the locomotive shed and goods shed and has lovingly restored and painted the signal box. The surrounding countryside is as fertile, productive and prosperous as ever, but has forgotten the railway. Only a few relics and some fading personal memories remain.

CHAPTER 3

Railwaying on a Shoestring

While it is obvious that lost branch lines have died as a result of changing demands for transport, it is less obvious that even when they enjoyed a near monopoly it was not always a golden age for them. In truth, many branch lines were in financial straits right from their inception. Many would never have been built had there been any alternative means of transport, or indeed if their building had been left to the initiative of the larger railway companies. In spite of the dense population and advanced economy of the English lowlands no network of secondary lines, either standard or narrow-gauge, emerged which was at all comparable with the *chemins de fer viçinaux* of Belgium. This was for a number of reasons, which included the high cost of obtaining Parliamentary authorisation for each line, and the high standards to which all passenger-carrying lines had to conform.

These costs made the larger companies reluctant to act, but local capital was often forthcoming to build branches as a means of opening-up isolated rural areas to economic development. Much of this capital was sunk without trace. The line would be promoted by a nominally independent company with local landowners and businessmen as directors, and would be worked by the main line company on fixed terms, irrespective of the traffic carried. All too frequently receipts fell far short of payments to the operator, which would subsequently buy out the local company at a considerable discount. The SER was particularly adept at this manoeuvre.

To encourage the building of rural branch lines the Railway Facilities Act was passed in 1870. It had little effect because, while cutting Parliamentary costs, it did not allow lines to be built 'on the cheap' by reducing technical standards. Much more successful was the Light Railways Act of 1896, under which a line could be authorised by a Light Railway Order made by the President of the Board of Trade (the Minister of Transport after 1919), thus saving the heavy costs of a Private Bill. In addition the stations, signalling and operating methods could be greatly simplified, thus reducing costs even further. The penalty exacted in return was a severe speed limit, tolerable in the days of the horse, but which ultimately was to play a large part in the decline of the light railway.

After 1896 a considerable mileage was constructed under Light Railway Orders, though by no means as great as expected by many of the Act's supporters. Many of these lines were electric street-tramways. Even though these sometimes achieved a segregated right of way, as did the Portsmouth & Horndean and the Isle of Thanet tramways, it was the classic double-deck British tramcar which rumbled over them into the open country. They were not the freight carriers of the Belgian *viçinaux*.

In our area, however, three lines are of particular interest, two of them having been built under the 1896 Act. Not only do they show all the features of the light railway, but they remained independent until either closure or nationalisation. Furthermore, they were chronically short of capital and were always operated on a make-do-and-mend basis. They also formed part of a very peculiar railway empire, the group of lines controlled by Colonel Stephens.

Colonel Stephens

The name is well enough known to railway historians and enthusiasts, but the Colonel remains a peculiarly shadowy figure. No biography of him exists and railway history has concentrated on the lines he managed to the exclusion of the person of the manager and of his policies.

Lt-Col Holman Fred Stephens, TD, M Inst CE, was born in 1866, the son of a well-known art critic. After studying mechanical engineering at University College London, he served an apprenticeship in the Neasden workshops of the Metropolitan Railway. Later he turned to the civil engineering side, becoming Resident Engineer for a number of railways. He supervised the building of 340 route miles in all, including in our area the Cranbrook & Paddock Wood (Chapter 2), the Sheppey Light Railway (Chapter 6) and the Rye & Camber (Chapter 9). He was also responsible for the rebuilding to passenger standards of the Burry Port & Gwendraeth, and the Plymouth, Devonport & South Western Junction Railways. He was also associated with the direction and management of light railways. His obituary notice in *The Railway Gazette* of 30 October 1931 says of him: 'latterly he had been prominently associated with eleven light railway undertakings of which six, totalling 112 miles are on the standard gauge, three totalling 49 miles are on the 1ft 11½in gauge, one, the Rye & Camber, is 3ft gauge, and the Snailbeach is 2ft 4in gauge.'

His army experience was as a Territorial with the Royal Engineers, and at one time he commanded the Kent (Fortress) Battalion of that Regiment, stationed at Dover. But he is chiefly remembered for his management of a group of light railways which he controlled from an office in Salford Terrace, Tonbridge. The group consisted of the three lines in our area, the East Kent, the Kent & East Sussex, and the West Sussex, and in addition, the Weston, Clevedon & Portishead (Somerset) and the Shropshire & Montgomeryshire, together with the little Shropshire mineral line, the Snailbeach District. He also for a time managed the Festiniog and Welsh Highland Railways.

These lines were beloved of enthusiasts for their miscellaneous and antique collections of rolling stock and their complete individuality, unaffected by the rising tide of standardisation which marked the 'Grouping Era' of 1923–47. Colonel Stephens is regarded as a rather quaint eccentric, perhaps in some ways anticipating the activities of the railway preservation societies. He could, however, be regarded as an innovator in rural transport. It is true that he was collecting light railways at a time when other enterprising transport men were collecting the rural bus services which eventually became the 'territorial' companies, only in the 1970s lapsing into the uniformity of the National Bus Company with its choice of two liveries. But his approach could be seen as a correct one towards rural rail transport. It involved minimal capital expenditure on the track, stations and signalling, at a time when the ordinary branch line was thoroughly over-capitalised, and further savings through the purchase of second-hand rolling stock. It also involved minimising the heavy labour requirements of the orthodox rural lines. Operating and engineering staffs were minimal, and there were less closely-drawn lines of demarcation in the duties they carried out. There was a flexibility of approach to operating, commercial and staffing problems often lacking in large companies. He thus provided a freight service at reasonable cost to rural areas, which possibly could still be given. His failing was probably the image projected by the general air of delapidation. This was the attraction for the railfan, but was the bane of the regular traveller, who would much have preferred the smart new omnibuses.

The East Kent Railway

The rolling chalk downland of East Kent might be considered an unlikely area to conceal a coalfield beneath it, but geologists suspected the presence of coal because of structural affinities with parts of Belgium and Holland known to contain the mineral. The first boring put down to prove their theories was at Dover in 1890. (The statement sometimes repeated by railway historians that coal seams were discovered during construction of Lydden Tunnel by the London, Chatham & Dover in 1860–1 is a myth.) The first colliery was on the seashore at Shakespeare Cliff, the

Headcorn
5. Kent & East Sussex Railway Terrier 0–6–0T No 3 disposes of the wagons brought in by the 15.50 train from Robertsbridge after arrival at Headcorn on 15 July 1939, the journey described on page 43.
6. The up platform at Headcorn in 1974. The right-of-way of the former Kent & East Sussex line to Tenterden bears away to the right.

7. A surviving Terrier 0–6–0T, No 32678 of St Leonards depot, assists a returning hop-pickers' friends' excursion past Junction Road on its way from Bodiam in 1958. A sister locomotive heads the train at the far end.
8. In 1974 rails were still laid at the site of the East Kent station at Shepherd's Well and used to store wagons waiting to be taken to Tilmanstone Colliery.

shaft being sunk in 1896. Both it and the later pits at Chislet, Snowdown and Betteshanger were located alongside or near existing railway lines. But coal also lay beneath the railwayless area bounded by the Dover–Canterbury East, Dover–Minster and Minster–Canterbury West lines.

The two firms (one British and one French) concerned with developing the coalfield applied for a Light Railway Order to permit them to provide rail access. Order No 361 was granted on 19 June 1911, incorporating the East Kent (Light) Railways Company and authorising a 10¼ mile line from Shepherd's Well (on the LCDR line from Canterbury East to Dover) to Richborough, with a six-mile branch from Eastry to Wingham. Later Orders authorised short branches to collieries and eighteen miles of line were opened on 16 October 1916. By 1918 130,000 tons of coal were carried annually.

The East Kent took full advantage of the relaxation permitted by the Act in the requirements for costly equipment. They provided the simplest of stations, a short ash platform edged with timber or brick, and a 'bus-stop' shelter. Train control was by telephone between block posts and fixed signals were few. The rails were flat-bottomed and spiked directly to the sleepers, while ballasting was minimal.

The East Kent made a junction with a siding on the down side of the SECR 250yd north of Shepherd's Well station. The line curved sharply, throwing off a short spur to the two-road passenger station, which adjoined that of the SECR. Like all East Kent stations, amenities were spartan, ash-surfaced platforms and a single one-storey building which served as waiting room, booking office and the headquarters of the line.

The line traversed the highest part of the Downs by a long deep cutting and the ¼ mile Golgotha Hill tunnel. Colonel Stephens, who was engineer, general manager, locomotive superintendent and had a seat on the board, inserted an arched brick roof for double track, but only excavated enough below for a single line, so that the cost of any eventual doubling would have been greatly reduced.

Emerging from the cuttings through high ground, Eythorne station ($1\frac{3}{4}$ miles) was reached and thereafter the line ran over the surface of the land with virtually no earthworks. Eythorne was a passing place and from it a two-mile branch ran southward to serve the short-lived and unsuccessful collieries at Coldred and Guilford. Apparently the line was still *in situ* when Klapper and Dalston described the East Kent in *The Railway Magazine* of March 1937, though officially closed in 1927. Northwards from Eythorne was a shorter branch (in fact a loop off the 'main line') running through Tilmanstone Colliery. The line up to the north end of the loop was in use for coal until the miners' strike of 1984–5 and the subsequent uncertainty about the colliery.

The line then struck northward past a halt ($2\frac{1}{2}$ miles) serving the colliery village of Elvington, Knowlton ($3\frac{1}{2}$ miles) and Eastry South Halt ($5\frac{1}{2}$ miles), each with a siding, to reach Eastry ($5\frac{3}{4}$ miles). This was optimistically described as being for Sandwich, which town was over two miles away and well served by the SECR and later even better by the Southern Railway.

Eastry had a passing loop, single platform and siding and was the junction for Richborough. The site can just still be distinguished. The 'main line' then curved sharply round from north-east to north-west. Just beyond was a short branch to Hammil colliery, which ended up as a brickworks still in production. Woodnesborough ($6\frac{1}{2}$ miles) had a siding and Ash Town (eight miles), Staple ($8\frac{3}{4}$ miles) and Wingham Colliery ($10\frac{1}{2}$ miles) were each equipped with a loop. Wingham Colliery was the original terminus though in the event the mine never actually produced any traffic.

The East Kent Railway never succeeded in reaching a town of any size, nor indeed any considerable source of traffic other than the mines, but in 1920 it obtained powers for various extensions totalling $26\frac{1}{4}$ miles. One such was from Wingham Colliery to a junction with the SECR line between Canterbury West and Sturry. One mile of this eventually went into service, circling Wingham village and with a station at Wingham Town. The line crossed the A257

Canterbury–Sandwich road on the level and ended just the other side, precisely nowhere, at Canterbury Road ($11\frac{1}{4}$ miles). Trains were pushed into a trailing siding on the other side of the road and after the locomotive was released they were allowed to run back by gravity.

Richborough stands at the mouth of the Stour where it enters Pegwell Bay. It developed as a military port during World War I (see p 132). The East Kent's $4\frac{1}{4}$ mile line from Eastry was built to enable coal to be exported from Richborough and figured as one of a series of unsuccessful attempts to revive this port after the war.

Half a mile north of Eastry was Poison Cross Halt. Beyond ($1\frac{5}{8}$ miles) was Roman Road (Woodnesborough) Halt. At Sandwich Road ($2\frac{1}{2}$ miles) on the A257, well over a mile out of town, the mixed train, which ran over the branch twice on Saturdays only, left its coach behind and went on to Richborough to deliver or collect any freight traffic. The weekly passenger service ceased on 31 October 1928 and the freight service was extremely desultory thereafter. The line crossed over the SECR and made an end-on connection with the port lines. Here was Richborough Port Halt, which never had a passenger service. The port lines connected the East Kent with the SECR spur about a mile to the north. The track ran alongside the A256 Sandwich–Ramsgate road, crossing it on the level several times.

Although this part of Kent is closely settled for a rural area, the East Kent never went anywhere that passengers would want to go, and apart from miners few were carried. By 1927, 24,957 workmen and 4,588 ordinary third-class passengers travelled. By 1938, the latter figure had fallen to 838, less than three per working day! In 1925, there were three round trips (one extra SO) from Shepherd's Well to Wingham Colliery, with short workings to Eastry (one SX, two SO) and to Eythorne (two SX, one SO). Frequency gradually fell away, but in spite of the almost total absence of traffic, two mixed trains (each with a single passenger coach) operated on weekdays until 30 October 1949.

In 1935, 7,048 tons of general freight, and 2,118 tons of 'other minerals' and 336 head of livestock were conveyed on the mixed trains. But the mainstay of the line was the 240,796 tons of coal, coke and patent fuel from Tilmanstone Colliery. The small quantities of general freight ceased to be carried beyond Eastry in 1950 and over the whole line the following year. But a diesel shunting locomotive still made several trips a day to Tilmanstone until 1 March 1984.

In 1939, the motive power fleet consisted of six more-or-less active locomotives. No 2 *Walton Park* (Hudswell Clarke 0–6–0ST 823 of 1908) was purchased from the Weston, Clevedon & Portishead Railway in 1917. At various times, from the SECR and the Southern Railway came the following 0–6–0s: No 6—ex-372, in May 1923; No 8—ex-A376, in September 1928; No 100 (later No 2)—ex-1383, in May 1935; and No 1371 (not renumbered) in March 1944. No 5 was ex-LSWR Adams 4–4–2T No 0488, which came to the East Kent from the Railway Operating Division in April 1919. No 7 was former LSWR Beattie 0–6–0ST E0127. No 4, a Kerr Stuart 0–6–0T was bought from the Inland Waterways & Docks Department (a wartime government organisation) in 1919. After 1939, the line was worked by O1 class 0–6–0s based at Dover, until the introduction of diesel shunters.

The Kent & East Sussex Light Railway

Chapter 2 examined the nature of the country in the angle between the Tonbridge–Ashford and Tonbridge–Hastings lines and how this was eventually penetrated by the Hawkhurst branch. But one Wealden market town, Tenterden, remained unserved, although there was a proposal in 1864 for a branch from the Hawkhurst line at Cranbrook.

In 1896 the Rother Valley (Light) Railway was incorporated to build a line from Robertsbridge on the Tonbridge–Hastings line of the SER to Tenterden. The latter was a small market town; there was no industry, and the line would serve a purely agricultural area. A Light Railway

Order was obtained in the same year, making use of the new Act. The line was opened as far as Rolvenden, for freight on 29 March 1900 and for passengers on 2 April. The short extension to Tenterden Town went into service on 15 April 1903. In that year a Light Railway Order was obtained for an extension to the SER Tonbridge–Ashford line at Headcorn and another Order the following year altered the name of the company to Kent & East Sussex Light Railway. The Headcorn extension opened on 15 May 1905 and there the line ended, though plans were drawn up and a suitable locomotive bought for a further extension to Maidstone (Tovil Goods).

The line started from a short bay at the London end of the down platform at Robertsbridge. There was a long run-round loop, but no sidings other than the SECR goods yard on the down side. The line curved sharply round the village to cross the A21 on the level. Just beyond, the only private siding on the line trailed-in from a flour mill.

The line ran along the floor of the well-wooded Rother Valley, passing the latterly almost unused Salehurst Halt (1⅛ miles) to cross the Junction Road, a well-engineered turnpike dating from 1844 and now the A229 from Hawkhurst to Hastings. Just beyond the level crossing was Junction Road Halt (2½ miles), optimistically described as being for Hawkhurst (four miles). There was a siding here, used for traffic to and from the nearby Guinness hop farms. Bodiam (3⅞ miles) was the first station. Situated adjacent to the inevitable gateless crossing, it was typical of the line, a short platform and a wooden building containing a waiting-room and booking-parcels-goods office. The lean-to roof was carried over the platform and given a deep, white-painted fascia board. There were three sidings but no passing loop. Just beyond the station the line passed close to the castle. In the early days the company had its eye on the tourist traffic. Northiam (approximately 6¾ miles) was the next station. Similar in situation and appearance, it had a loop and two sidings. Even in the 1950s there was quite a significant coal traffic here and at Bodiam.

The line then crossed the low-lying Rother Levels, an

embayment of Romney Marsh, to reach Wittersham Road station (9¼ miles), located three miles along narrow lanes from the village. There were no gates on the crossings of the main roads at Junction Road and Northiam, but on the almost deserted lane on which the station stood, the crossing had gates. There were two sidings.

The next station was Rolvenden (12¼ miles), considerably nearer Tenterden than it was to Rolvenden, the nearest station to that village being Wittersham Road. It was all very complicated. Rolvenden station was virtually devoid of traffic, but was important as being the headquarters of the line, with locomotive depot and workshop. There was a passing loop, just west of the short platform, and five sidings which in 1939 were filled with the most incredible collection of junk and scrap.

Here the line left the marshes and climbed steeply at 1 in 52 round a sharp curve up to Tenterden Town (13½ miles). It was on this bank that the 'Terrier' tanks hauling the seven-coach 'Wealden Limited', which was the final passenger train over the Hawkhurst and KESR lines on 13 June 1961, ran short of steam and stuck for nearly half an hour. Tenterden Town was the largest and busiest station, conveniently situated just behind the main street. It had a more substantial building of brick on the westbound platform, a passing loop and five sidings which were usually well filled.

The line continued its climb to St Michael's Halt (15¼ miles) and just beyond passed through a short tunnel, the only major engineering work. The country is now high, more rolling and much less wooded. High Halden Road (16½ miles) was for a change less pessimistically named, the centre of the straggling village being scarcely more than a mile away; there were three sidings. Biddenden (nineteen miles) was nearly a mile from the village, but in true KESR style, the line had already skirted close by it. Biddenden had a siding and a passing loop, usually used for storing wagons. The last station before Headcorn was Frittenden Road (twenty miles). It was inconveniently located, and even in

1939 its platform and sidings were deserted and grass-grown. At Headcorn (twenty-two miles) there was a long platform forming a 'V' with the up SR platform. They were both slightly re-sited when fast lines were provided through Headcorn in 1924. There was a connection with the SR up loop line on the London side of the station. The KESR accommodation consisted of two loops and a siding.

The author re-discovered notes of a journey he made on Saturday 15 July 1939. He travelled down to Robertsbridge on the 14.25 Charing Cross to Hastings, formed of an SECR non-corridor 'long set' of nine coaches hauled by a Schools 4–4–0. The KESR train, the 15.50, consisted of locomotive No 3, an ex-LBSCR Terrier 0–6–0T, and an ex-LSWR non-corridor brake composite coach. It left with eight passengers, while the brake was filled with parcels. Tickets were inspected and also sold to local passengers by a porter who walked along the footboards from compartment to compartment while the train was in motion. The riding was rough and bumpy, and looking ahead only the tops of the rails could be seen through the weed growth. But looking out was hazardous, for the uncut hedges continually scraped the sides of the coach. The ungated crossings were protected only by 10mph signs, the train driver slowing to about that speed, with the locomotive whistling continuously.

At Bodiam the travelling porter left (he was the staff there), together with two passengers. Another left at Northiam, two at Wittersham Road and the remaining two at Tenterden. Only the author travelled beyond. At Rolvenden the 16.25 from Tenterden Town was passed, hauled by another Terrier in Southern black and numbered 2655 and consisting of one coach similar to ours.

A booked wait of twenty-five minutes at Tenterden was reduced to one of only a few minutes by a late arrival. The staff seemed to consist of a porter and a boy. There had been one man at the other stations, the halts being unstaffed. In the yard was the company's road vehicle, a delivery van. The train left Tenterden with three passengers. At Biddenden one got off and another got on. A loaded wagon and nine empty ones were picked up. They were trailed behind the coach without refinements such as brake-van or tail lamp. At Frittenden Road someone got on, so four passengers were decanted at 17.50 on Headcorn station where the author caught the 18.00 stopping train to Tonbridge.

If this was typical, then it was surprising the passenger service lasted as long as it did. The returns for 1920 show how limited the traffic always had been. There were 1,552 first-class passengers, 65,816 third-class, and no workmen. That represents five first-class and 230 third-class passengers per weekday. It is tempting to speculate who the eight season ticket holders were and between which stations they travelled. Perhaps they were commercial travellers, for the time table would scarcely allow commuting. On the freight side 7,661 tons of general merchandise were carried (about twenty-five tons per day), and 4,318 head of livestock, mainly sheep from Biddenden autumn fairs. Then, as always, domestic coal was the principal traffic, amounting to 43,764 tons. In that year the train mileage was 28,000. All the steam trains were mixed, freight wagons being attached as required. From 1923, however, these were supplemented by a peculiar unit, two model-T Ford buses coupled back-to-back, a bold pioneering experiment in cost-cutting, but they were said to have given a very rough and noisy ride.

The 1925 timetable showed the line being worked as virtually two sections, from each terminus to Tenterden Town (which involved light running between there and Rolvenden). There were five departures from Robertsbridge (two by railcars), with a further railcar trip WO. From Headcorn there were four departures (one by railcar), with an extra railcar TuO. As the years went by there was little change, though the railcars had disappeared by 1935. Gradually the emphasis shifted to the Headcorn section, presumably because most of the traffic was between Tenterden and London and this was the quicker way. Between 1928 and 1933, however, a through coach for Tenterden was provided on the 17.12

from Cannon Street (17.20 from Charing Cross SO) to Hastings, which was detached at Robertsbridge.

The 1954 timetable gave three departures from Robertsbridge and five from Headcorn, a rare example of an increase in service in the later years of branch lines. It was possible to leave Tenterden at 08.00 to arrive at Cannon Street at 10.14 and to return on the 17.40 to reach Tenterden at 19.52, via Headcorn in both cases, but it would have been quicker to drive to Headcorn to join the main line train.

At the outbreak of the war in 1939 both the KESR and the East Kent Light Railway came under the control of the Railway Executive and the operation of both lines was integrated with that of the Southern; thus they passed to the British Transport Commission under the nationalisation measure of 1947. During the war the line was relaid to provide an alternative route if others were closed by bombing. The Southern worked it with O1 class 0–6–0s, a practice which persisted until 1954.

The passenger service lingered on until 4 January 1954, when the Headcorn Extension was closed completely and torn up two years later. Freight continued on the Rother Valley section until 12 June 1961. Terrier tanks, shedded at St Leonards, were used until Drewry diesels took over in the latter years. Hop-pickers' specials were operated as far as Bodiam until 1959. On Sundays a six-coach corridor train would make a trip with a Terrier at each end.

After closure the track remained down and a preservation group was formed. The group planned to operate both passenger and freight trains from 1965. Unfortunately its efforts were frustrated by the refusal of the Ministry of Transport to permit running across the A21. The stream of cars and lorries thundering through the narrow street of Robertsbridge could on no account be interrupted, not even two or three times a day. However, the Society gathered an interesting collection of stock at Rolvenden and the other stations. It was eventually decided to seek a Light Railway Order to re-open the line between Tenterden Town and

Bodiam, and in 1973 the line was re-opened between Tenterden Town and Rolvenden as a first step. Later, services were extended to Newmill Bridge and in 1984 to Hexden Bridge, five miles from Tenterden Town station.

Hawthorn Leslie built two 2–4–0Ts in 1899 for the new line. No 1 *Tenterden* and No 2 *Northiam*. In 1901 Terrier No 70 *Poplar* was bought from the LBSCR, renamed *Bodiam,* and given the number 3. Transferred by BR to the Hayling Island Branch, it has since returned to Rolvenden. In 1903 Hawthorn Leslie supplied *Hecate,* an 0–8–0T, for the proposed Maidstone extension. It was too heavy and was sold to the SR in June 1932, ex-LSWR Beyer Peacock 0–6–0T being received in part exchange. Both carried the number 4. Number 5 was another Terrier, No 671 *Wapping,* which was bought in 1905 and renamed *Rolvenden.* Number 6 was an unsuccessful steam railcar obtained in 1905 from R. & Y. Pickering. Number 7 *Rother* was ex-LSWR Ilfracombe Goods 0–6–0 No 0349, bought in 1910. There was also No 9 *Juno,* another former LSWR 0–6–0 No 0284, bought in 1914. Finally, there were the twin Ford railcars of 1923 and a similar unit built by Shefflex in 1930. Mention must also be made of the 1848 LSWR Royal Saloon sold to the Plymouth, Devonport & South Western Junction Railway in 1890 and later transferred to the KESR as an inspection saloon. But in the 1930s it was often used in ordinary service. All these were scrapped between 1934 and 1945, except Nos 3 and 4. The former is back on the line, under the auspices of the Tenterden Railway. The saloon is at York Museum.

The West Sussex

There is a contrast in the coast east and west of Brighton. Eastward stretch the chalk cliffs, but westward a low, flat coastal plain, gradually getting broader, separates the lower slopes of the South Downs from the sea. West of Worthing the Brighton–Portsmouth line runs well inland and the coastal resorts served by branch lines. Those to Littlehampton, Bognor and Portsmouth are anything but forgotten.

The Hayling Island branch is dealt with in Chapter 6. The last branch ran from Chichester to Selsey.

The Hundred of Manhood & Selsey Tramway was incorporated on 29 April 1896 to build a 7¾ mile line from Chichester to Selsey across the low-lying coastal plain, no point of which exceeds 20ft above sea level. It was built by private arrangement at a cost of £21,000 and opened on 27 August 1897. It was extended for half a mile to Selsey Beach on 1 August the following year, though this section fell out of use about 1906. No legal powers were obtained until the West Sussex (Selsey Tramway Section) Railway Certificate was issued in 1924 under the Railway Construction Facilities Act of 1864.

Construction and equipment were of the simplest. The single track was of rails spiked direct to sleepers with little or no ballast. By the final years of operation the joints were badly aligned and the track had disappeared under weeds two or three feet high. The riding of the Shefflex railcars was thus noisy and rough. The line followed the level surface of the land and was almost devoid of earthworks. There was only one overbridge, but six level crossings, unprotected by anything but 5mph speed restriction boards. There were no signals, no gradient posts and no mileposts. The only intermediate passing loop was at Sidlesham and only there and at Hunston were there crude shelters on the platforms.

The West Sussex yard at Chichester adjoined the Southern station to the south. It had a delapidated station with one platform, a loop, three sidings and a connection with the Southern goods yard. The line swung southward across open country, the station then being on the southern outskirts of the town. The first station was at Hunston (2¼ miles) with a siding and a water crane. Next came a private halt serving Hoe Farm and then Chalder station (3¾ miles), with a siding. This was also named after a farm but was the nearest stop to Sidlesham village. Mill Pond halt was reached at 4½ miles and the most important intermediate station with loop and siding at Sidlesham a half-mile beyond. Another half-mile further on was Ferry Siding Halt (with a siding as its name implies). Between those two stops the line crossed an arm of Pagham Harbour by the 'Tramway Bank', the only major earthwork. Golf Course Halt ($6\frac{1}{2}$ miles) and Selsey Bridge Halt ($7\frac{1}{4}$ miles) followed, and finally Selsey was reached. This was the most pretentious station. Its single platform had a small waiting room and parcels office. There was a loop, two sidings, a locomotive shed and a shed for the railcars.

There were five locomotives. Number 1 *Selsey* was a Peckett 2–4–2T built in 1897 for the opening of the line. Number 2 *Sidlesham* was a Manning Wardle 0–6–0ST of 1861, bought in 1907 from Blagden Waterworks. Number 3 *Chichester* was an 0–6–0ST built by Hudswell Clarke in 1903 and bought in 1911. Originally No 4, it replaced the original *Chichester* which was an 0–4–2T built in 1847 as an 0–6–0T for the GWR from which it was bought in 1897. The later No 4, *Morous,* was a Manning Wardle 0–6–0ST of 1866 transferred about 1926 from the Shropshire and Montgomeryshire. Number 5 *Ringing Rock* was an 1883 Manning Wardle 0–6–0ST. There was also an 0–4–2ST *Hesperus* (No 2) built by Neilson in 1872 and bought in 1912 from the PDSWJR. Only *Chichester, Morous* and *Ringing Rock* were working in 1935. In addition there were two twin Shefflex railcar units similar to the one on the KESR. Two LCDR six-wheelers were the only usable coaches at the end.

In the summer of 1934 there were seven departures from Chichester and six from Selsey, with an extra round trip on Wednesdays and Saturdays. All but one service was operated by the railcars. In *The Railway Magazine* of 1935 there was a description of a journey from Chichester made in September 1932 by the daily mixed train. This was made up of a six-wheeled coach and some coal wagons hauled by *Morous*. The author of the article was the only passenger; a faster and more comfortable bus service had paralleled the line since 1919. Some of the wagons were left at Hunston and an empty one picked up at Chalder. It was small wonder the line closed to all traffic on 19 January 1935.

CHAPTER 4

Secondary and Local Lines across the Wealden Hills

The High Weald figures largely in this account of the forgotten railways of South East England (see also Chapters 1 and 2). Its parallel ridges separated by deep and steep-sided valleys have an east-west trend and so lie athwart routes from London to the South Coast. Until the twentieth century it was an area of backward farming, small, remote market towns and sparse population. It was a barrier, both physical and economic, rather than a source of traffic.

Even today the intensive development which has swept over the South East since World War II is, as far as the Weald is concerned, confined to the corridors of movement provided by the main roads and railways crossing the area en route from London to Brighton and the other coastal towns. The principal corridor and the main axis of development is, of course, the electrified Brighton line, the parallel A23, and the M23.

Elsewhere the High Weald lacks any large centre of population, apart perhaps from Tunbridge Wells, and has very little industrial activity. It is still very rural, though so popular with wealthier commuters that property prices soar sky-high. It is not the sort of country to generate large-scale local traffic; commuters drive to railheads on the main lines where there are intensive services, and there are no sources of freight to support the train-load-based operations of the modern railway. It must of course be remembered that there never was enough traffic to enable its railway lines to function profitably.

The High Weald was, and still is, an area of great natural

beauty, with wooded rolling hills, narrow hedge-bound lanes winding through meadows, orchards and hop-gardens, and infrequent but attractive villages and small towns built of warm red bricks or of timber frames. Through these quiet scenic backwaters the branch lines never had more than local importance, but they survived almost intact until the 1960s, even experiencing vastly improved train services in the 1950s. However, they had no place in the scheme of things we associate with the Beeching–Marples era, and they suffered very severely, being more severely pruned here than anywhere else in the area covered by this book.

To understand more easily the rise and decline of the Wealden lines, the Brighton line has been taken as a convenient division. In this chapter we will turn first to the area lying to the east, a square-shaped area bounded by four main lines, the Brighton line itself, the 'Coastway East' line from Brighton to Hastings, the Hastings–Tonbridge line and the Tonbridge–Redhill line.

The defence of Brighton

The LBSCR route from London Bridge to Brighton was opened throughout in 1841. The Company's East Coast line reached Lewes from Brighton in 1846 and Eastbourne in 1849. The SER opened its main line from Redhill to Tonbridge in 1842, and the line onward from there to Hastings finally opened ten years later.

Though there were a number of schemes for branches penetrating the High Weald eastward of their main line between Redhill and Keymer Junction, there is little doubt the LBSCR would have been content to leave things as they were, especially as it was in grave financial difficulties. But to settle for the status quo was subject to an important proviso—that the SER would reciprocate. For Brighton was the main prize for the LBSCR and there were no other major sources of traffic beyond Croydon. The preservation of their monopoly at Brighton was the overriding consideration. To this end the

LBSCR entered into an agreement with the SER, dated 10 July 1848. Ostensibly it regulated the tolls charged by one company on the other's traffic over the London Bridge–Redhill line, owned in part by each company. In fact it was a territorial agreement, settling spheres of influence. The full story of the agreement and its gradual breakdown is told in 'Southern England'.

The final breakdown came with the fierce quarrels attending the opening of the Caterham Railway in 1856, though even before that peace between the two companies was very uneasy. The LBSCR felt that it had to defend its Brighton monopoly from the SER. Attack was the best form of defence, and the line of attack was to ensure that SER could not build south-westward from Tunbridge Wells. The traffic desert between Brighton and Tunbridge Wells was to be 'occupied' and the latter built up as a forward strong-point in the defence of Brighton. Instinctively one looked for an inscription on the portal of the West Station repeating Marshal Pétain's defiance of the German army at Verdun—'They shall not pass'.

On 18 June 1846 a branch was authorised to East Grinstead from Three Bridges, a locality (for there was no village of that name) on the line to Brighton, but nothing further was done. It was not until 8 July 1853 that the East Grinstead Railway was incorporated to build the line, the result of local initiative taken to provide the thriving market town with a rail connection. Hitherto, the nearest station was that of the SER at Godstone, seven miles north on the turnpike road (now the A22). The seven-mile branch line was opened for all traffic on 9 July 1855.

Another penetrating branch was promoted by an independent company to connect the market town of Uckfield with the LBSCR East Coast line at Lewes. The line was opened on 18 October 1858 from Uckfield Junction, 1½ miles north of Lewes on the Keymer Junction line, and ran for nearly 7½ miles up the Ouse Valley to Uckfield. The LBSCR quickly took over the independent companies.

The two lines were both pointing at Tunbridge Wells, thirteen miles from East Grinstead and $15\frac{1}{2}$ miles from Uckfield. The LBSCR was anxious to close these gaps and hastened to support local companies promoted for the purpose. The East Grinstead, Groombridge & Tunbridge Wells Company was incorporated in 1862 and opened its $13\frac{1}{2}$ mile line on 1 October 1866. The other gap was closed by the Brighton, Uckfield & Tunbridge Wells Company, incorporated in 1861. Its line, opened on 3 August 1868, was just over twelve miles long and extended from an end-on junction at Uckfield to the East Grinstead line at Groombridge Junction, a quarter-mile west of Groombridge Station. Both companies were taken over by the LBSCR even before the lines were opened. It should be noted that all the branches were single-track, an indication of the sparse traffic expected.

Brighton was now secure. The London Chatham & Dover had deposited a Bill in 1864 for a Beckenham–Brighton line, but the LBSCR did not take any serious notice. For now it was the turn of their Eastbourne interests to be threatened, since the SER had also deposited a Bill for a Tunbridge Wells–Eastbourne line. To counter both these moves the Brighton Company also introduced a Bill, for a proposed Ouse Valley Railway. This would have run from the main line south of Balcombe down the Ouse Valley near the sites of Ardingly and Sheffield Park stations and then through Uckfield and East Hoathly to Hailsham. There a connection would be made with the line opened on 14 May 1849 from Polegate on the 'East Coast' main line.

The LBSCR obtained powers for the Ouse Valley, the LCDR effort proved abortive, while the SER was persuaded to withdraw on condition that a connection between its Central Station and the Brighton's West Station at Tunbridge Wells was built. A daily freight train used the spur from 1867, but the Brighton Company delayed introducing a passenger service until 1876. Work started on the Ouse Valley line, but though the distance to Eastbourne would have been shortened, the duplication of the route already existing

Then and now at Barcombe
9. Summer time in the Sussex Weald provides the background for a typical Wealden station and train. Only the BR livery dates the scene when the 14.59 from East Grinstead was photographed as it left Barcombe on 2 September 1953. Such a train could have been seen at any time after the formation of the SR in 1923 brought LBSC locomotives and SE&C coaches together. *(R. C. Riley)*
10. Barcombe in 1974. 10a. Barcombe in 1983.

11. SR West Country class 4–6–2 No 34100 *Appledore* heads a Ramblers' Club Victoria-Heathfield special up the climb towards Mayfield on 1 October 1961. This line was normally worked in its latter years as part of a complex interval timetable covering services between Victoria, Oxted, Tunbridge Wells, Eastbourne and Brighton. *(D. T. Cobbe)*

12. LMS-type 2–6–4T No 42103 with the 11.21 from Three Bridges to East Grinstead calls at Grange Road on 28 May 1955. The ex-SE&C 'Birdcage trio C' sets were in common use on Kent and Sussex main and branch services right up to the 1962 Kent Coast main line electrification. *(J. S. Gilks)*

through Lewes would have made the line hopelessly uneconomic.

But the LBSCR pressed on, and in 1865 obtained authority for an extension from Hailsham to St Leonards. At the time, the Surrey & Sussex Junction Company, with Brighton backing, was authorised to connect Croydon with Tunbridge Wells by a line via Oxted. The SER reacted furiously to what they considered to be a breach of the agreement reached over its Eastbourne venture, also harking back to the outdated 1848 Agreement. The LBSCR countered by calmly asserting it was only shortening its routes in the same way as the SER was doing by promoting its Sevenoaks line. The SER swallowed its pride and joined with the LCDR to obtain an Act for a London, Lewes & Brighton line.

The financial crisis of 1866 was perhaps a blessing in disguise. It brought all activity on the Ouse Valley and the Surrey & Sussex Junction to a halt. In the case of the Ouse Valley this was permanent, though some of the earthworks can still be traced. Undoubtedly the LBSCR, which had taken over the Surrey & Sussex, hoped that this line could also be permanently abandoned. The London & Brighton scheme remained stillborn.

As was so often the case, it was left to local initiative to bring about desired improvements in transport. In 1873 local business interests promoted a Bill for a 3ft 0in gauge line from Tunbridge Wells to Polegate. The SER became interested, and the scheme developed into one for a standard gauge line between Tunbridge Wells and Eastbourne. Little progress was made in raising the required capital and the Brighton stepped in, obtaining in 1876 an Act enabling it to take over the powers for a payment of £8,534. The Brighton now had authority to build on from Hailsham to Eridge on the Uckfield–Groombridge Junction line. As well as the cash, the SER was given a share in the Eastbourne receipts, and given running powers between Tunbridge Wells West and Eastbourne. In fact the rights were only exercised between April 1884 and December 1885 when two trains a day each way were put on between Charing Cross and Eastbourne via Tunbridge Wells West and Hailsham.

The $7\frac{1}{2}$ miles of single track were opened between Hailsham and Heathfield on 5 April 1880 and the $9\frac{3}{4}$ miles on to Eridge on 1 September of that year. The last $1\frac{1}{4}$ miles from Redgate Mill into Eridge paralleled the single track of the Uckfield line. When the latter was doubled in 1894 the Heathfield line north of Redgate Mill became the down road, a junction and signal box being provided at that point. The Heathfield line was always known to railwaymen as the 'Cuckoo Line', and often a train was referred to as going 'down the Cuckoo', perpetuating the old Sussex legend that the first cuckoo of summer was released at Heathfield Fair, held annually in June.

In 1878 powers had been obtained for a single-track spur one mile long between Ashurst Junction on the East Grinstead–Groombridge line and Birchden Junction, one mile north of Eridge. This enabled Groombridge to be by-passed without a reversal there. It remained unused, except to store condemned locomotives, until after the Oxted and Groombridge line had been opened. The spur was eventually doubled.

In the same year, 1878, a nineteen-mile line was promoted jointly by the Brighton and SER to run from the main line at South Croydon to East Grinstead, making use of the uncompleted right of way of the Surrey & Sussex Junction. At Crowhurst North Junction a spur climbed up to Crowhurst Junction South on the SER Redhill–Tonbridge line, allowing through running towards Tonbridge. North of Crowhurst North the line was jointly owned; south thereof the LBSCR was the sole owner. The whole line opened on 10 March 1884.

A number of local residents, including the Earl of Sheffield, launched the Lewes & East Grinstead Company. Their original scheme included the line north of East Grinstead, but they were asked by the LBSCR not to seek a Bill for this line. Their Act of Incorporation was dated 10 August 1877.

The Company was amalgamated with the LBSCR in the next year. The line made an end-on junction at East Grinstead and extended southward for $17\frac{1}{4}$ miles to Culver Junction on the Uckfield line, three miles north of Lewes. The line was opened on 1 August 1882, although the station buildings were not finished.

Meanwhile, the LBSCR obtained an Act on 19 July 1880 for a line connecting the Lewes & East Grinstead at Horsted Keynes with the more-or-less parallel Brighton main line at Copyhold Junction. The $3\frac{1}{2}$ mile line was opened on 3 September 1883. The East Grinstead–Horsted Keynes–Copyhold section was double, but that between Horsted Keynes and Culver Junction was single. The name 'Bluebell and Primrose' or just 'The Bluebell' became popular during the disputes of the 1950s, but the author was never aware of its use among railwaymen before that.

Although, like the South Croydon and East Grinstead, it is by no means a forgotten line, mention must be made of the Oxted & Groombridge's line, 12.13 miles from Hurst Green Junction on the East Grinstead line to Ashurst Junction. It was opened on 2 January 1888 as far as Edenbridge Town and on to Ashurst Junction on 1 October.

The passenger-train services

The train services evolved to satisfy local needs; short journeys to market, shopping or school, together with visits for business or pleasure to London, Brighton, Tunbridge Wells and Eastbourne. Apart from those to Tonbridge, where connection could be made with a variety of services, trains were not advertised to go further than the places mentioned. The only other exception was a daily service put on by the Southern between Brighton and Chatham via Uckfield, Tonbridge and Maidstone East, which ceased in 1939. Even that service was in fact only a reflection of the extensive and complex stock workings which were a feature of the SR. It was possible to travel from Brighton to Reading via Uckfield,

Tonbridge and Redhill in the same train, though it was not advertised as a through service.

While for operating convenience trains used to wander down from Victoria or London Bridge to the coast or to Tunbridge Wells, they were unlikely to carry any through passengers, who would be expected to travel by the more direct routes. In later years at least there were no through fares. In 1953 the author was unable to purchase a ticket at Victoria for Brighton via Uckfield though he was travelling by a through train. He was given one to Uckfield and had to pay the excess at Brighton.

Though at first the frequencies were sparse, they gradually built up after 1890 and this encouraged long-distance commuters. Large houses in large gardens spread first along the Oxted line to East Grinstead, especially around Warlingham, Woldingham, Oxted and Lingfield Stations. The heights around Crowborough and Forest Row also became popular, where from an early date suburban sprawl of very low-density housing foreshadowed that accompanying the motor age in North America. Even before 1914 wealthy commuters used cars to get them to the stations. In the inter-war years the trend continued, though now it was the timber-framed farmhouses and cottages that became popular. One day in 1946 the author was surprised to see how many cars were parked at Cowden Station. The trend continued after the war and small houses began to be built in and around the villages.

In the High Weald these villages are usually on the ridge tops, while the railway kept to the valleys and tunnelled under the narrow ridges. The stations were therefore inconveniently situated for the most part, travellers being faced with long uphill walks to the villages. The centre of West Hoathly was 220ft above the station. The tendency to have double-barrelled station names, Newick & Chailey, Crowborough & Jarvis Brook, Waldron & Horeham Road for example, indicated locations equally remote from both the named villages. Other stations served no villages at all, Sheffield Park and Barcombe Mills among them. Yet others, such as Hellingly and Buxted, were named after insignificant settlements. Because of this, most of the short-distance traffic between the wars was lost to the buses which used the ridge-top roads and passed through village centres. The improved post-war train services were mainly used by London commuters and day visitors to London and the other larger towns.

In 1865 there were nine trips to East Grinstead and six to Uckfield. These services were eventually projected on to Tunbridge Wells West. Service levels increased very slowly. In 1885 there were twelve down weekday trains to Oxted. Five of these were LBSCR trains for East Grinstead and beyond via the 'Bluebell Line', while three SER trains ran over the Crowhurst spur. There were six trains from Three Bridges to Tunbridge Wells, which shared the line beyond Groombridge with seven trains from the Uckfield line and five from the 'Cuckoo'.

By 1904 the services had assumed a pattern which was to remain without radical change until 1933. Basically a service was operated between London and Brighton via the 'inner circle' through East Grinstead or by the 'outer circle' through Edenbridge Town and Uckfield. Between Oxted and Hurst Green Junction there were now forty-six down trains against the eight in 1885. Fourteen were SER trains proceeding via the Crowhurst spur. A further twenty were 'inner circle' trains. The remaining twelve went round the 'outer circle' in whole or part.

Beyond East Grinstead the 'inner circle' service was complex. Most of the through trains from London continued on to Brighton via Sheffield Park and Lewes, but two or three reached Brighton via Ardingly and Copyhold Junction. There were also some trains between East Grinstead and Brighton via Ardingly and some short-distance workings between Horsted Keynes and Haywards Heath.

The 'inner circle' through Oxted and Ardingly was regarded by the LBSCR as an alternative route to Brighton especially before the widening of the main line, which was completed in 1907 as far as the north portal of Balcombe

Tunnel. The 'inner circle' was regularly used by excursion trains and even after electrification steam-hauled trains used it in emergencies. During the war Horsted Keynes signal box was manned continuously because of the stategic importance of the line as an alternative route.

From Three Bridges to East Grinstead there were twenty trains daily. Most ran through to Tunbridge Wells, but a few turned back at East Grinstead or Forest Row. Through services from London were very rare. From 1888 the 17.05 London Bridge–Eastbourne slipped a portion at Horley, which was worked forward to Forest Row, but because of increasing patronage this service in Southern days was replaced by a complete train leaving London Bridge at 17.09. This was withdrawn in 1939 and never reinstated after the war.

The 'outer circle' was worked in two sections. All twelve down trains were for Tunbridge Wells except a late working which terminated at Edenbridge Town. These connected at Groombridge with trains originating at Tunbridge Wells West, ten for the Uckfield line to Brighton and eight for the 'Cuckoo' and Eastbourne. There was a total of eighty-three workings between Groombridge and Tunbridge Wells West, but the spur on to the Central Station was used only by four round trips made by SER trains. In 1914 the Birchden Spur was opened to regular traffic. By 1925 there were six down trains over the spur, four to Brighton and two to Uckfield. Three carried through portions for the 'Cuckoo', which were detached at Eridge.

After 1923 the new Southern Railway made few changes. Greater use was made of the Tunbridge Wells spur by projecting some of the trains from Brighton on to Tonbridge. By 1925 there were seven trains each way over the spur and by 1934 these had increased to twenty. On the other hand their use of the Crowhurst spur declined. In 1925 there were two up services but no balancing down ones. One of these lingered on until 1955. But the spur was regularly used by excursions and hop-pickers' specials. It was also used as a diversionary route for main line trains via Tonbridge when Polhill or Sevenoaks tunnels were closed for maintenance work.

Electrification of the main line in 1931 meant that through trains from the 'inner circle' no longer worked beyond Haywards Heath. The 1935 electrification programme included the Copyhold Junction–Horsted Keynes section. The hourly service from Seaford via Lewes and Keymer Junction was projected on to Horsted Keynes; the reason given for electrifying from Copyhold Junction was that reversing the multiple-units at Haywards Heath would cause congestion; we were expected to believe that the Southern's planners had never heard of a reversing siding.

Meanwhile, interrupted only by the war, business traffic increased steadily, and train weights increased up to the limits imposed by the severe gradients. There was, however, little change in the train services except that more trains went to Tunbridge Wells via East Grinstead, with connections at Oxted for the Edenbridge line. In the 1930s the milk traffic transferred to road, but on the 'inner circle' the unchanged timetable forced long waits at stations to handle the non-existent milk-churns. Freight traffic was always light and gradually declined; all that remained was coal and a few tons of general freight. One or two lightly-loaded pick-up freights each day on the various sections were all that was necessary to cater for this traffic. The main goods depots were Oxted, Edenbridge Town, East Grinstead, Heathfield and Hailsham. The other stations handled little more than the occasional wagon of coal.

In July 1952 there were twenty-three departures on Mondays to Fridays from Victoria or London Bridge for destinations beyond Oxted. Four were routed down the old 'inner circle' via Sheffield Park to Brighton. Six reached Tunbridge Wells West via Edenbridge, while one terminated at Groombridge. Six reached Tunbridge Wells via Lingfield and East Grinstead, and two went no further than East Grinstead. Many of these had connections at East Croydon, Oxted or East Grinstead for other destinations. Finally five trains used the Birchden spur; three conveyed Uckfield and 'Cuckoo' portions and dividing at Eridge; the 16.40 from London Bridge was for Uckfield only; while the 16.50 from Victoria to Brighton carried a Tunbridge Wells portion which was detached at Ashurst, the only occasion in the day that station was used to divide trains.

The author travelled on the 11.08 from Victoria one Saturday in that July, the train consisting of a three-coach non-corridor ex-SECR set (a 'Birdcage-trio C') and a four-coach SR corridor set of flat-sided stock usable on the Hastings line (an E-set). It was hauled by a Brighton-built 2–6–4T of the LMR class 4 series, known for some reason to Southern men as 'Teddy Bears'. Eridge, with its two island platforms, was reached at 12.14. A few minutes later a train bringing passengers from Tunbridge Wells arrived, a 'Birdcage-trio C' set hauled by L class 4–4–0 No 31771. Almost at the same time the 11.19 Brighton–Tonbridge came in to provide a connection for Tunbridge Wells. At 12.18 the 2–6–4T with the front set left for Eastbourne down the 'Cuckoo'. Number 31771 left its coaches and backed on to the rear E-set leaving for Uckfield and Brighton at 12.24 to arrive at the latter at 13.35. This was a typical working in later steam days.

In June 1955 an interval service, reinforced in business hours, was introduced on the lines north of East Grinstead and Groombridge. The package included the decision to close that part of the 'inner circle' between East Grinstead and Culver Junction. No towns or large villages were served, and objections by the East Grinstead Urban District Council were met by providing an hourly shuttle service from East Grinstead to Three Bridges, connecting there with southbound services. Services were advertised to cease on 13 June 1955, but due to the ASLEF strike the last train ran on 28 May. However, a clause in the Agreement between the LBSCR and the Lewes & East Grinstead Company guaranteed West Hoathly, Horsted Keynes, Sheffield Park and Newick & Chailey stations four trains a day. This enabled local residents to force BR to re-open with effect from 7 August

1956. British Railways kept to the letter of the law. Four round trips were made at times when nobody wanted to travel, and they did not stop at Barcombe, which had developed into the busiest station. The farce continued until an Act could be obtained to allow closure from 17 March 1958. Looking back from the post-Beeching Era we wonder what all the fuss was about.

The story of the 'Bluebell' was not, of course, over. A preservation society was formed and re-opened the line between Horsted Keynes and Sheffield Park in 1960. Since then it has gone from strength to strength. The line north of Horsted Keynes was kept on a care-and-maintenance basis and used for wagon storage until 1960. The Bluebell Railway now has ambitious plans to link up again with British Rail at East Grinstead, re-opening the line north of Horsted Keynes.

In June 1956 the interval service was inaugurated on the southern part of the system. The whole service revolved around a train leaving Victoria at eight minutes past the hour for Tunbridge Wells West via Oxted and East Grinstead. At Oxted a connecting pull-and-push service left for Tonbridge via Edenbridge Town and Tunbridge Wells. At Groombridge passengers for the South would make a second change. After a few minutes wait a train from Tonbridge to Brighton via Uckfield would come rattling in, followed five minutes later by one from Tunbridge Wells West to Eastbourne via the 'Cuckoo'. Soon after the through train from Victoria would call at Groombridge, having connected at East Grinstead with the shuttle from Three Bridges. All lines had an hourly service, eight trains called at Groombridge every hour, and fifty-eight passenger trains and two freights used the Tunbridge Wells spur daily, making it, for most of the year, the busiest stretch of single track in the country, yielding that honour to the Isle of Wight on summer Saturdays.

For the motorised railfan it was possible to wait on Crowborough station listening to the beat of the locomotive coming up the 1 in 80 with a Tonbridge to Brighton train, watch it into the station, then, driving not too dangerously to Rotherfield, to repeat the exercise with the following Eastbourne train.

Decline

The new service attracted much new custom. Meanwhile, the Hampshire lines were next on the list of dieselisation. It is very hard to speculate what would have happened if the Beeching Report of 1963 had not been published and converted into tablets of stone. In 1965 a survey revealed there were on average 250 passengers a day on the 'Cuckoo', but surprisingly only twenty-three season ticket holders. The immediate effect of the Beeching programme was to put a stop to the efforts to foster traffic. In addition, it is hard to resist the impression that the Southern Region was forced to contribute its share of the one-third of the total mileage to be closed, and that it selected non-electrified routes, which in fact meant the Wealden lines. Meanwhile, electric services to Horsted Keynes ceased from 28 October and only a siding retained from Copyhold Junction to a freight depot at Ardingly. Apart from the Crystal Palace High Level branch it was the only significant 'Southern Electric' closure.

In 1964 the interval-service timetable was recast. This partly reflected changes in traffic flow. But instead of the close connections through the whole system which characterised the 1958 timetables, there were now long waits, designed to deter passengers from using the services on the lines scheduled for closure. On 14 June 1965 the 'Cuckoo' was closed to passengers north of Hailsham. Freight trains ran from Hailsham to Heathfield until 26 April 1968, when a bridge sustained damage and was not repaired. Hailsham was closed completely on 9 September 1968 and with it disappeared the last stretch of the 'Cuckoo', from Polegate to Hailsham. The Three Bridges–Ashurst Junction line was closed completely on 2 January 1967 except for East Grinstead passenger station and the section from Three Bridges to an oil depot at Rowfant. This lasted for some years. The line was then abandoned and the route has been completely severed by the M23 motorway.

There was more difficulty over the Uckfield line. The British Railways Board sought complete closure south of Ashurst and Groombridge Junctions. But after vigorous opposition from local authorities and private individuals the Minister allowed closure only between Uckfield and Lewes (exclusive). The date of closure was fixed as from 6 January 1967. The Traffic Commissioners, however, deferred licensing the replacement buses. The Southern engineers then pronounced the viaduct across the Ouse at Lewes to be safe only for one line. A shuttle service was put on between Lewes and Uckfield, for the revised timetable had already been issued for the line north of Uckfield. The engineers then insisted the viaduct must be closed on 23 February. Accordingly the Southern hired buses. Barcombe Mills and Isfield booking offices remained open to issue tickets, but since the buses could not get up the long road approach to Barcombe Mills, a taxi was provided to take the passengers down from station to bus-stop, presumably after they had walked up to buy their tickets. The substitute Southdown buses finally started on 6 May 1967. Future railway historians will have many furious debates as to the exact closure date. But in the 1920s a thousand tickets would be collected on Bank Holidays from anglers alighting at Barcombe Mills.

Description of the Lines

Trains left for East Grinstead from a short bay at the country end of the down fast platform at Three Bridges. The single line immediately curved away to the east, climbing at 1 in 88 for 1½ miles into the forest Country of the High Weald. Rowfant (2½ miles) was the first station and was a passing place; Grange Road (four miles) the next one had no crossing facilities. Both were named after nearby country houses and Rowfant remained very isolated. Grange Road attracted a small settlement which has grown considerably since the closure of the line. Where a by-road crosses at six miles is the site of Imberhorne Siding, provided for the nearby Manor house.

East Grinstead ($7\frac{3}{4}$ miles) had high- and low-level platforms at right angles to each other. The high-level section was on the Three Bridges–Groombridge line and had two island platforms. It could also be reached from the Oxted direction by the double line spur up from St Margaret's Junction opened on 10 March 1884, the same day as the line from South Croydon Junction via Oxted to the end-on junction with the Lewes & East Grinstead. The latter had two low-level platforms opened on 1 August 1882. The main buildings

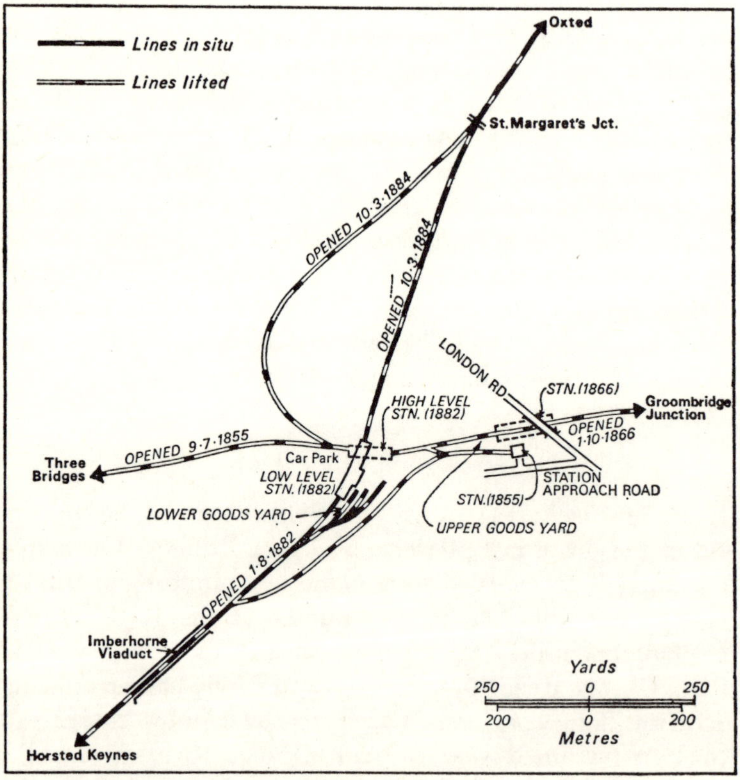

East Grinstead

were on the down low-level platform, and have been rebuilt. The high-level section is now a car park, all trains using the low-level platforms. The present station is the third. The first, opened on 9 July 1855, lay immediately to the east and still survives as a dwelling, though the Inner Relief Road now runs along the former railway. This station was replaced on 1 October 1866 by the second station (used until October 1883) at the London Road bridge and slightly nearer the town centre. Coal sidings at the low-level station were reached by a single-line spur (used only for freight and empty stock trains) from the second station.

The line on to Groombridge descended steeply from East Grinstead into the Medway Valley at Forest Row, a crossing place 3¼ miles to the east. Forest Row is a large but scattered village and the station was inconveniently sited. The run down the Medway Valley was very pretty. Before the opening of the Edenbridge Town line, the LBSCR tried to popularise this roundabout way to Tunbridge Wells as 'The Pleasant Route'; that at least was no exaggeration. Hartfield (6¾ miles from East Grinstead) and Withyham (eight miles) were small stations rather inconveniently sited for the villages they served. The right-of-way is part of *The Forest Way*, a 'greenway'. The line from Edenbridge Town was joined at Ashurst Junction (9¾ miles).

From East Grinstead Low Level the line to Lewes, double to Horsted Keynes, descended over the ten-arch Imberhorne Viaduct. Lines are still laid over the latter to serve as reversing sidings for the diesel-electric multiple units operating the Victoria–East Grinstead service. The grade then steepened to 1 in 75 down to Kingscote (two miles), yet another station named after a nearby house and described by R. C. Riley in 1954 as being 'almost entirely devoid of both passenger and freight traffic'.

The next station was West Hoathly (3·88 miles from East Grinstead). It was a considerable exercise in hill climbing to walk from station to village. South of the station the line plunged into the 730yd West Hoathly Tunnel, inclined at

1 in 75 against up trains and notoriously wet and slippery. The line descended the side of a valley of a tributary of the Ouse to Horsted Keynes station, 6²/₅ miles from East Grinstead and a hilly 1¼ miles from its village. The station had five platform faces and four through roads. The electric trains terminated at one face of the outer platform; the fourth track had then been taken up. Ironically it was the platform which had been deprived of all shelter. The sidings alongside were used at intervals to store condemned locomotives and coaches. Like all stations on the line the main buildings at Horsted Keynes were of a very plain design and built of red brick. Large platform shelters were provided supported on wooden pillars. The station is now used by the Bluebell Railway and has been extensively reconditioned. There are plans to extend the Bluebell to East Grinstead.

South of the station the double track to Copyhold Junction bore away westward. The bridges, of red brick, were particularly substantial. Ardingly station and yard, which were a long way from the village, have been developed as a railhead for aggregate traffic and are very busy. The station buildings, attractively restored, have become the offices, and the depot is reached by a single-track spur from Copyhold Junction.

The Lewes line south of Horsted Keynes was always single. It is still in active use as far as Sheffield Park, (4·38 miles), now the headquarters of the Bluebell Railway. The station has been restored to give a fine impression of a Victorian country station; this and the yard filled with rolling stock of great interest is well worth a visit. The halts between Horsted Keynes and Sheffield Park were provided by the Bluebell.

The now abandoned road-bed climbs out of the Ouse Valley to Newick & Chailey, equally remote from both villages and 6¼ miles from Horsted Keynes. The crossing facilities had been removed many years before closure. Beyond the 63yd Cinder Hill tunnel the line switch-backed across low hills to Barcombe Mills (9¾ miles) which never had a crossing place.

Just over a mile beyond the station the double-track line from Uckfield was reached at Culver Junction. This had pursued an uneventful course down a broad fertile valley through Isfield and Barcombe Mills. The original line went on to join the Keymer Junction–Lewes line at Uckfield Junction. But on 1 October 1863 a new $3\frac{1}{2}$ mile approach to Lewes was opened. It left the old line at Hamsey about $1\frac{1}{4}$ miles south of Culver Junction. Trains could now reach Brighton without a reversal at Lewes.

North of Hamsey the integrity of the right-of-way was preserved at the request of the East Sussex County Council. In addition some of the Ouse valley earthworks can be

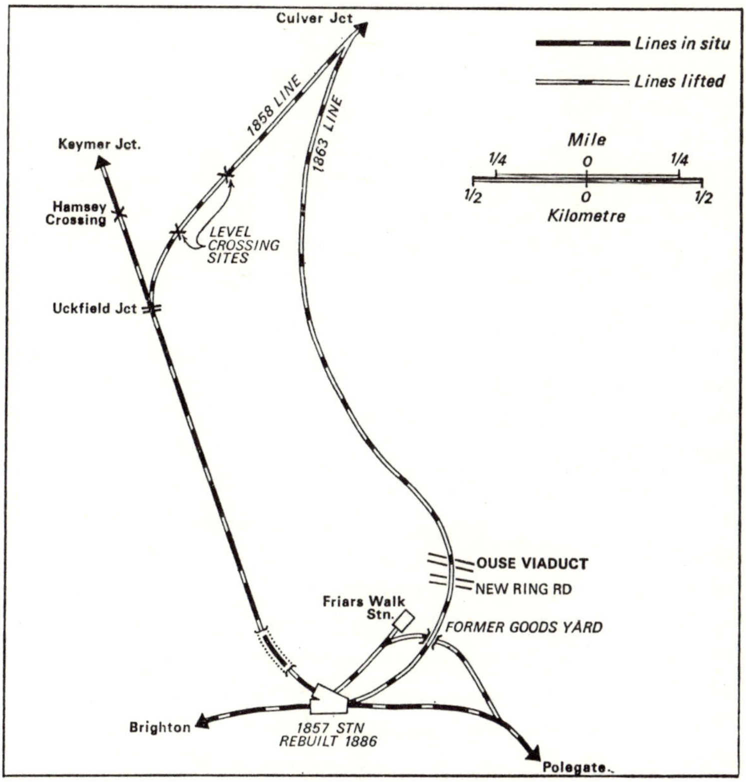

The Lewes area

traced. The 'new line' south of Hamsey has very largely disappeared; the Ouse viaduct has gone and the section beyond obliterated by the new Lewes inner ring road. Oddly enough, the 'old' line is more easily traced.

The 'Cuckoo' left the Uckfield Line at Redgate Mill Junction, remotely situated in a narrow valley 1·38 miles south of Eridge. It was single throughout with passing places at all the stations. A feature of several of them was the absence of a signal box. The frame and token instruments were on the platforms in the open, surrounded by an iron fence. Otherwise they looked much like all the stations in the area: the nominally independent companies apparently employed the LBSCR architect.

It was a very stiff climb up through the woods to Rotherfield ($1\frac{3}{4}$ miles from Redgate Mill) and on to Mayfield ($2\frac{5}{8}$ miles from Rotherfield). Both stations were inconveniently situated and had little traffic, though Mayfield milk depot had a private siding and despatched milk tanks until about 1950. From Mayfield it was a long undulating and beautiful run of $3\frac{3}{4}$ miles to Heathfield. This was conveniently sited to serve a large scattered village of the same nature as Forest Row and Crowborough. It had the heaviest passenger traffic on the line, for it served as a railhead for a wide area. It had a large goods depot and was distinguished by being lit for some years before World War I by natural gas, from a well sunk nearby. The gasholder could be seen just by the tunnel mouth to the north of the station.

The line descended through Waldron and Horeham Road station ($2\frac{1}{2}$ miles from Heathfield). Waldron was $2\frac{1}{4}$ miles away; Horeham Manor was nearby. After World War II the Southern more realistically renamed it Horham after the small settlement which had grown up around the station. Hellingly, the next station and $3\frac{5}{8}$ miles to the south, formerly boasted a private siding worked by an electric locomotive which used to take wagonloads of coal and stores to the large hospital. Traces of this line can still be found.

Hailsham, $1\frac{4}{5}$ miles beyond, was conveniently sited to serve

13. New uses for old stations. The platforms of Rotherfield station form convenient sides for a swimming pool, and the platform awning the roof of a sun lounge.
14. The original East Grinstead Station (1859) survived in 1974 and in Station Road.

Then and now at Baynards
15. The 17.04 pull-and-push train from Guildford leaves Baynards on 7 April 1956. *(J. S. Gilks)*
16. Baynards in 1975; it is still possible to walk the right-of-way.

the small but flourishing market town, rather overshadowed by Eastbourne. It had a large goods depot and was the terminus of short workings from Eastbourne sometimes worked by main-line locomotives filling-in time. Finally the line crossed flat agricultural land to reach the main line at Polegate Junction.

In our area there was no closure for some sixteen years after 1969. But then in 1983 notice was given of closure of the $4\frac{3}{4}$ miles between Grove Junction (Tunbridge Wells) and Birchden Junction. This involved withdrawing the hourly shuttle service between Tonbridge and Eridge, where connection was made with the Uckfield trains, and closure of the West and Groombridge stations.

The proposal was fought strongly and the TUCC recommended retention but closure took place on 7 July 1985. As a condition of closure, a bus, sponsored by BR and East Sussex County Council, operates between Tunbridge Wells Central and Groombridge.

There were some disconcerting implications. In pursuing immediate gain from selling the extensive West station site, BR 'adjusted' the estimated savings. Was it part of a scheme to get the Uckfield line closed? Certainly bookings south of Eridge declined significantly. However in 1986 BR announced not only long-term retention of the line but substantial investment aimed at modernisation and cost-saving.

Only a few lines would then penetrate the area, the electric one to East Grinstead, the preserved Bluebell line, and the 'Lavender Line'. The latter is a private venture dating from 1983. Track was laid northward from the restored Isfield station. The integrity of the right-of-way north of Lewes was maintained for some years as the local authorities pressed for re-opening. But even with changed public if not political attitudes towards railways, it is unlikely this part of the Weald can offer incentives for further restoration of services.

CHAPTER 5

West of the Brighton Line

The story of forgotten railways in the Weald to the east of the London–Brighton main line can be told as a coherent whole, but that of forgotten lines to the west of the main line is much more fragmented. Closed lines are scattered and there is no single theme in the story of their rise and decline.

In the first place, fewer lines were built in the area, probably because the danger to the LBSCR monopoly of Brighton traffic was not under such constant threat from the north-west as it was from the north-east. In the second place, the 'Mid-Sussex' line (Dorking/Three Bridges–Horsham–Arundel Junction) has always had a main line status, similar to that of the Tonbridge–Hastings line, a status which no line between the latter and the Brighton line ever achieved.

The terrain, landscape, and economy of the Weald westward from the Brighton line were, and are, similar to those in the eastern Weald described in the previous chapter, though there are some subtle minor differences. In the wide stretch of country between the Redhill–Guildford line to the north and the West Coast line, from Brighton to Chichester and Havant, to the south the only place of consequence is still Horsham. Even in 1971 it numbered only 26,446 souls, and in the mid-nineteenth century only some 5,000.

The Mid-Sussex Line

Although of course the Mid-Sussex is still very much in being, with a basic passenger service of at least one train an hour each way, a brief reference to its history will help us to bring the description of the other lines into perspective.

The main line to Brighton was opened in 1841, while the West Coast line from Brighton to Portsmouth was completed in 1847. The LBSCR now had a route between London and Portsmouth $95\frac{1}{4}$ miles long. This was competitive while the LSWR ran via Eastleigh, but ceased to be with the opening of that company's Portsmouth Direct line from Guildford in 1859. But the Mid-Sussex line, which shortened the distance for the LBSCR to eighty-seven miles was not planned as a Cut-off. The LBSCR later developed it as one, but it grew in a haphazard and piecemeal fashion. The full story is told in 'Southern England' (p 104 *et seq*). The first line in the area was that from Three Bridges to Horsham, opened in 1848. The railway reached Dorking from the north in 1859, and was opened thence to Horsham in 1867. The line onward from Horsham to Hardham Junction went into service in 1859 but as part of the line to Petworth (p 83), not to the coast. The Mid-Sussex route was not completed until 1863, when the gap between Hardham Junction and Arundel Junction on the West Coast line was closed.

From Shoreham to Horsham

The route leading inland through the South Downs by means of the Shoreham Gap, created by the River Adur, is an easy one. It was chosen by several of the unsuccessful schemes for a London–Brighton railway, including that promoted by Robert Stephenson. In the event a more direct route for that line was selected, traversing the barrier of the South Downs by means of Clayton Tunnel.

But the Shoreham Gap was still an attractive route. In 1857 a railway was promoted by Joseph Locke and Thomas Brassey to reach Shoreham Harbour from Dorking, via Horsham. In the likely event of LSWR support forthcoming it would constitute a challenge to the LBSCR monopoly at Brighton. That company therefore countered with a scheme to link its West Coast line at Shoreham with the Mid-Sussex at Itchingfield Junction, just over three miles south of Horsham. In a Parliamentary struggle the LBSCR emerged victorious, its Act receiving the Royal Assent on 12 July 1858.

The line, seventeen miles long in all, was opened from Shoreham to Partridge Green on 1 July 1861, thence to Itchingfield Junction on 16 September. Originally single, the line was doubled throughout between 1877 and 1879. It formed part of a possible through route from London to Brighton, 61½ miles long from Waterloo and 63¾ from London Bridge. In fact it never developed as such, unlike the 'inner circle' via Ardingly, and the passenger service was always only a local one, going no further than Brighton and Horsham. As such it pursued a placid, uneventful path until final closure. It was a typical Victorian country branch with no outstanding features. It never had other than local passenger and freight functions, and when these ceased to exist, it no longer had a purpose.

Shoreham Junction, a quarter-mile west of Shoreham station, was the beginning of the line which curved away northwards from the Portsmouth line and downward to the west bank of the Adur. The A27 was crossed on the level ¾ mile north, at the end of the old wooden toll-bridge. The tolls were owned by the railway and the crossing-keeper collected them. The railway, road and river now ran side-by-side through the deep gap across the South Downs. Here a small marshalling yard was laid in during the last war. Two and a half miles from Shoreham Junction was Beeding Cement Works, now the terminus of a siding from Shoreham. Crossing the river, the line struck across the water-meadows to the first station at Bramber (3⅞ miles), a small roadside station. The line curved round below Bramber Castle to reach Steyning (4⅝ miles), a picturesque small market town of 3,245 inhabitants in 1971. The station was distinctly peripheral, but it was the most important on the line for both passengers and freight. The weekly market was held adjoining the goods yard and in earlier days was a considerable source of traffic.

North of Steyning the valley opens out, with the scarp of the Downs away to the South. The line ran through low-lying meadows to the next station, Henfield, on the very edge of a large and scattered village, 8½ miles from Shoreham Junction. Beyond Henfield the line crossed the Adur for the last time and struck away into the hillier, more wooded High Weald. But it is an area which even before the motor age would have provided little traffic. Partridge Green, two miles beyond Henfield, served only a very small village. West Grinstead, another 2⅝ miles beyond, was over a mile from the locality of that name. Southwater, 2⅞ miles north had a similar catchment area, but the adjacent brickworks had a private siding which at one time did bring some traffic on to the line.

Itchingfield Junction, seventeen miles from Shoreham and 1½ miles beyond Southwater was a lonely signal box, remote from any road, where the line joined that from Arundel Junction. The junction station was at Christ's Hospital, ¾ mile to the north. It is an odd station, opened in 1902 to serve housing developments which never took place. It is named after the nearby school. Clearly traffic at the spacious station never came up to expectations. There were seven platform faces and five through tracks. The main buildings were on the down side, the platform served by a long loop off the down main line. Next was an island serving the down loop and down main, then was a 'V' platform serving the up main and down Guildford line. Finally, there was an unnecessary island between the up and down Guildford tracks (see below). Recent rebuilding has reduced the number of platforms in use to two, facing the up and down main lines.

Christ's Hospital was not a terminal point; the trains started from and terminated at Horsham. In the same way, at the southern end, they all ran through to Brighton. The service varied little over the years. In 1930 there were thirteen departures for Horsham from Brighton with one or two short workings to Steyning. The service was increased after the Mid-Sussex electrification of 1938 and in 1960 there were seventeen weekday departures from Brighton to Horsham with a late working to Steyning, a very adequate and perhaps over-lavish service.

In the author's extreme youth he was dragged complaining on to the bus at Horsham to travel on to Steyning, it even then being regarded as more convenient. He would have much preferred to travel in the motor-train, of one or two big 'balloon' cars pulled or pushed by a tiny D1 0–4–2T. Not until 1953 was he able to travel the line, by the 16.58 from Brighton one Saturday in July. A flat-roofed ex-LBSCR motor set was hauled by an ex-LSWR M7 0–4–4T. The well-filled train emptied considerably at Steyning, but after that no one got on or off at any of the next four stops until at Christ's Hospital about twenty passengers descended to wait for the Guildford train. The train from Brighton reached Horsham at 18.03 with only a handful of people on board. It was more surprising that the line had survived so long than that it had no place in the post-Beeching era. The elimination of steam workings from Brighton led to dieselisation in May 1964, but the costly diesel-electric units could be better employed elsewhere. By then virtually all the freight traffic had been lost apart from that to and from Beeding Cement Works. With little opposition the line closed completely from 7 March 1966, except that access from the south was maintained to the cement works.

Horsham & Guildford Direct

The Horsham & Guildford Direct Railway Company was incorporated in 1860 to build a 15½ mile single-track line from the Mid-Sussex line at Stammerham Junction to the Portsmouth Direct Line at Peasmarsh Junction. It was a grandiose name for a company set up by local enterprise to build an unimportant branch line. The new company started to construct the line, but before it was completed they sold out in 1864 to the LBSCR. The line was opened on 2 October 1865.

There was no station at Stammerham Junction, which was eventually the site of Christ's Hospital (West Horsham) station. Just beyond the station the line became single and curved sharply away to the north-west. When the line was first opened, a spur facing Itchingfield Junction was provided. It was rarely used and was closed on 1 August 1867.

The line undulated with quite steep gradients across the clay lands to the first station at Slinfold 2½ miles from Christ's Hospital, where there was a private siding to a brickworks. After crossing beneath the A29 (on the alignment of the Stane Street, a Roman road), the line crossed the upper Arun. Originally the bridge was a single brick arch, but the approach embankments were subject to slipping. They were reinforced, and a girder was put in 10ft above the top of the arch of the bridge.

The gradients became more severe, climbing at 1 in 80 into the forested hills of the central Weald through Rudgwick, the next station (4⅘ miles). The inspector delayed the opening of the station for a month until the grades through it were eased. The summit was reached in Baynards Tunnel, very wet and slippery. It brought many a freight train to a halt, including one hauled by a powerful Q1 0–6–0. Just over the summit Baynards (six miles) was reached. Though both Slinfold and Rudgwick had small goods yards, Baynards was the first crossing place, the sections being worked by staff and ticket. Besides a goods yard there was connection with a private rail system serving the fuller's earth plant.

Baynards was named after the nearby Baynards Park, the other two after small villages. Cranleigh (8⅞ miles) served the only place of any size, a large scattered village which during the inter-war years became a commuter centre. There was a small goods yard and a siding to a gas works. The line now ran almost straight and level down the Wey Valley. Alongside could be seen the remains of the derelict Wey & Arun Canal. Birtley siding served a county council depot a mile or so before Bramley Station ($12\frac{3}{4}$ miles) was reached. Like Cranleigh it had crossing facilities. It was conveniently sited for the small village.

The line now ran along the marshy floor of the Wey Valley. Where the Bramley–Guildford road (A281) was crossed there was a public goods depot at Stonebridge Sidings, near Stonebridge Wharf on the Wey & Arun Canal. Just before Peasmarsh Junction ($15\frac{1}{2}$ miles) the Wey was crossed by a bridge (now removed) which placed restrictions on the types of locomotives used. All Moguls, Pacifics, 4–6–0s and the heavier 4–4–0s were banned, but a Deltic diesel could have been taken over the branch had anyone ever wanted to do so. The line between Baynards and Peasmarsh Junction was divided at Cranleigh and Bramley into three sections and operated by electric train staff.

At Peasmarsh the branch trailed into the main line from Portsmouth. This was a short distance south of Shalford Junction where the Redhill line comes in. The remains of a spur which, had it ever been completed, would have provided a connection from Redhill to the Portsmouth direction, can still be plainly seen. The Portsmouth Direct line had been authorised in 1853. The company had been floated as a speculation principally through the efforts of Thomas Brassey. Neither the LSWR nor the LBSCR ever wanted much to do with it. An amending Act authorising the spur was obtained to tempt the SER, which virtuously would have nothing to do with the Direct line either. But it had the desired effect. The LSWR suspected that the SER's scruples might well be eventually overcome and agreed to take over the line.

Beside the normal local passenger and freight traffic on the Horsham & Guildford Direct there was commuter traffic from Cranleigh and freight from the private sidings, especially from Baynards. In the last few years of its life there were some eighty season ticket holders from Cranleigh, but by then most of the other traffic had been lost. At Rudgwick on many a day no tickets were sold after the 08.37 for Horsham had left. In 1948 8,162 tickets were collected at Baynards and in 1962 only 3,579 or under ten a day. There were few to enjoy the magnificent display of dahlias on the platform while waiting for their trains. The freight had declined disastrously especially after the 1955 strike. In 1948 there were 671 loaded wagons inwards at Baynards, while 802 were dispatched. A monthly train of sulphur for processing the fuller's earth came from Angerstein Wharf via Horsham until closure, but in 1962 only one loaded wagon was forwarded. All the goods yards were closed during 1962, parcels traffic ceased and there remained but a handful of passengers.

As so often happened, the train service appeared designed to deter rather than encourage passengers. Some services were timed to leave Horsham a few minutes before possible connections arrived, yet a fifteen-minute wait at Cranleigh was included to extend the time to sixty minutes for a 19½ mile journey. It was no surprise when closure proposals were announced in September 1963. There were the inevitable protests, but they were not strongly supported, and closure came on 14 June 1965. D. Sillence (*The Railway Magazine*, March and April 1966), from whose excellent article the author has drawn heavily, considered that passenger traffic could have been developed with an interval service giving good connections at Guildford and Horsham. Ironically, in the years since closure there has been considerable housing development around all the towns and villages between Guildford and Horsham.

Unlike the Shoreham line, the service dwindled over the years. It was always self-contained, Horsham and Guildford being the terminals, though there were short workings for commuters between Cranleigh and Guildford. The line was used quite frequently for through excursions. In 1930 there were eight weekday departures from Guildford to Horsham with an extra on Wednesdays and two (three on Saturdays) for Cranleigh. In 1939 there were nine weekday departures from Guildford for Horsham and three for Cranleigh. Of these latter the 19.16 was mixed, continuing as a freight-only to Horsham. On Sundays there were two departures for Horsham and two for Cranleigh. There were also paths for

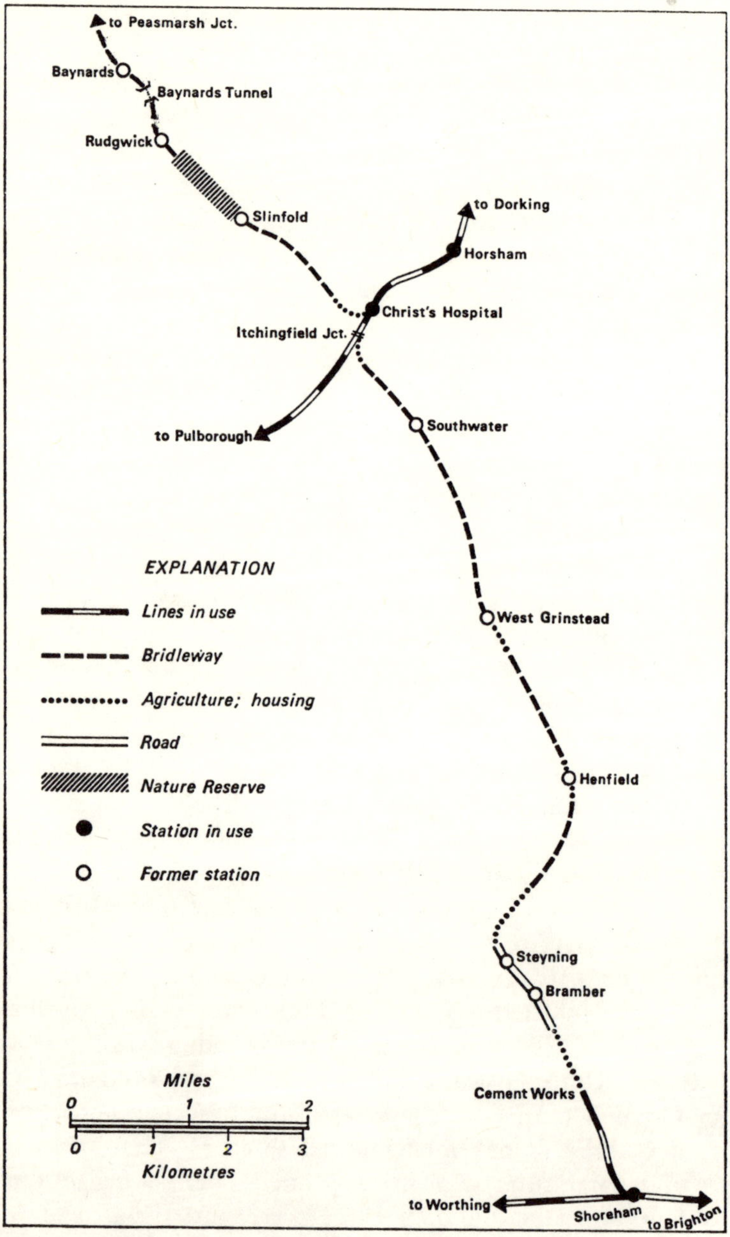

New uses for old railways: Shoreham–Baynards

seven excursion trains, such as Surbiton to Bognor and Windsor to Bognor. In 1960 there were nine Horsham departures (eight on Saturdays), but cuts were made soon after. The line was steam worked to the end, by M7 0–4–4T in Southern days, but by Standard class 2 2–6–2T in later years. Corridor sets were used for the most part in later years.

West Sussex County Council bought the right-of-way south of Baynards Tunnel, together with the Shoreham line as far as Steyning, while Waverley District Council took over the section north of the tunnel. A 'greenway', The Downs Link, now goes the whole way, the lengths of formation no longer available being by-passed and collapsed bridges north of Cranleigh repaired.

Rails to Midhurst

The headwaters of the River Rother rise beneath the chalk rim of the Weald west of Petersfield. The river flows eastward, winding along a broad valley until it joins the Arun at Pulborough. A line of villages is located along the spurs of higher ground on the northern slopes of the valley. One of these, Petworth, was the rather insignificant objective of the Mid-Sussex Railway, already referred to.

The company was incorporated on 10 August 1857. Its single line from Horsham through Pulborough and up the Rother Valley to Petworth was opened on 10 October 1859. The *West Sussex Gazette* gave a long account of the new line. It described the special train which left Three Bridges at 08.30 on 8 October 1859 carrying officers, reporters and the staff for the line: 'Men, women and children were being removed to a district which some of them had never seen before . . . and this train conveyed them to their destinations with their small collections of children, goods and chattels.' For an instant the curtain is drawn aside to give a glimpse of what the new railways meant for staff as well as customers.

As already recorded, the completion of the Hardham Junction–Arundel Junction section four years later meant that while the section north of Hardham was doubled and became part of the Mid-Sussex main line, west of Hardham remained an unimportant branch. The LBSCR worked the line and absorbed the company in 1864.

To extend the line beyond Petworth, the Mid-Sussex & Midhurst Junction Company was incorporated on 13 August 1859. The line was not completed until 15 October 1866, a very long time for 5½ miles through easy terrain. The local press noted the opening in sarcastic vein. The line was worked by the LBSCR but was not absorbed by that company until June 1874.

The Mid-Sussex & Midhurst wanted to build on up the valley to join the Portsmouth Direct line at Petersfield. But it was a client company of the LBSCR and the big company regarded such a step as a violation of its territorial Agreement with the LSWR. By the Agreement anything west of the route of the proposed Guildford, Chichester, Portsmouth & Fareham Railway of 1844 would be in LSWR territory. The Petersfield line therefore became the responsibility of the Petersfield Railway Company. Incorporated on 23 July 1860 it was amalgamated with the LSWR by the Act of 22 June 1863. The single-track branch was opened on 1 September 1864.

On 23 June 1864, Royal Assent was given to the Act empowering the Chichester & Midhurst Company to build a line between these places. The Brighton company was supporting the local company, and it suffered heavily in the financial crisis of 1866. We have already seen how this affected rails in the eastern Weald. Here too in the west, work came to a standstill. The projected extension from Midhurst to Haslemere was never started. The LBSCR obtained an Act in 1876 to revive the Chichester line, but it was not finally opened until 11 July 1881.

Midhurst thus became the focus of three branch lines. It is a delightful small town, with quite a large suburb at Easebourne, north of the river, but it had few industries and no modern factories. It was too small an objective for three railways through sparsely-peopled country.

Trains for Midhurst started from Pulborough on the Mid-Sussex which had a loop line and platform off the up line. There were also three water cranes on the platform ends, and a turntable. Hardham Junction was just under one mile to the south. It never had a station but was marked by a very old wooden signal box. Just west of Hardham the line crossed the Wey & Arun Canal. Fittleworth was the first station, $1\frac{4}{5}$ miles from Hardham. It was opened in 1889 and had a single platform and a siding, but there was no passing loop. Petworth was $2\frac{1}{2}$ miles beyond. While most of the villages lay north of the river, the line was built to the south. Petworth Station was sited where the line crossed under the A285 Guildford–Chichester road at a locality called Coultershaw Bridge, nearly two miles south of Petworth. It had a loop and small goods yard.

Selham, $2\frac{1}{2}$ miles beyond, was the only intermediate station. It had no passing loop, and dated from 1872. Just before reaching Midhurst (LBSCR), $3\frac{1}{2}$ miles to the west, the line traversed a short tunnel, which was the only substantial engineering work. The station, which was a passing place, dated from 1881, when the Chichester line was opened, and lay just west of the original station. To the west the Chichester line curved south while the connection with the LSWR went straight on past the LBSCR goods yard on the north side.

The LSWR station lay just beyond the bridge on the Bepton Road. The connection, owned by the LSWR, was brought into use on 17 December 1866 and used for transferring wagons by horsepower, as the bridge was too weak for locomotives. The public had to walk between the stations. Complaints were constant, but it was not until 12 July 1925 that the Southern concentrated passenger traffic on the LBSCR and closed the other station. The Bepton Road Bridge had been strengthened some time before. Freight traffic was concentrated on the Brighton company's depot.

The Petersfield line crossed Midhurst Common and bore away from the Rother. There were two intermediate stations, Elsted (3·38 miles from Midhurst) and Rogate ($5\frac{1}{2}$ miles), which were simple wayside stations with sidings, the latter having a loop. They were remote from anywhere, except for the hamlet of Nyewood, hard by Rogate station. Nine and a half miles from Midhurst (LBSCR) the line curved sharply round to join the Portsmouth line by a junction facing south. A terminal platform separated by a level crossing from the main station was provided for passenger trains.

The Chichester line branched off $\frac{1}{8}$ mile west of Midhurst LBSCR station, just before the LSWR yard was reached, and the A286 Midhurst–Chichester road which it closely paralleled through the South Downs all the way to Chichester. The first station was at Cocking ($2\frac{3}{8}$ miles) at the foot of the Downs. The line then wound through a narrow gap by a series of cuttings and three tunnels. Singleton station ($5\frac{1}{2}$ miles from Midhurst) was to be called West Dean, and lay half way between the villages. It was the station for Goodwood Racecourse, having four platforms and very extensive sidings to stable race trains. Lavant ($8\frac{5}{8}$ miles) was a railhead for sugar beet for over thirty years after closure to passengers, but the line now ends at a gravel pit $\frac{5}{8}$ mile to the south. The line joined the West Coast line at a junction ($11\frac{1}{4}$ miles from Midhurst), facing Chichester, which is controlled by Fishbourne Crossing signal box. It is $\frac{3}{4}$ mile west of Chichester, beyond the marshalling yard.

The train services were infrequent; the LBSCR ran between Pulborough and Chichester, though at one time there was a through coach for Midhurst slipped at Pulborough from the 16.05 from London Bridge. The LSWR ran a shuttle service between Petersfield and Midhurst. The Southern continued the practice of both companies. In 1930 there were nine trains each way between Pulborough and Chichester, with an extra round trip from Pulborough to Midhurst. There were also three Sunday trains as far as Midhurst. There were ten weekday trips from Petersfield to Midhurst (with no advertised connections there in Bradshaw) and three on Sundays.

Even then buses on the parallel road had eaten into the

limited Chichester–Midhurst traffic, and the section was closed to passengers on 6 July 1935. Freight traffic continued north of Lavant until 1953. Lavant was retained for seasonal sugar-beet traffic. In 1972 the remaining line took on a new lease of life. Aggregate was railed to the grading plant at Drayton 6½ miles away, thus saving Chichester City from a constant stream of heavy lorries. About five trains of high-capacity wagons are despatched daily.

After 1935 most trains ran through between Petersfield and Pulborough though with long waits at Midhurst. In 1929 there were nine trains (one extra WSO) from Petersfield to Midhurst. The author travelled the line only once, by a Sunday train from Petersfield in 1949. He and three companions were the only passengers all the way to Petworth, where they left the train. The Sunday service ceased in 1951, and all passenger services on 5 February 1955. The line west of Midhurst was completely closed, but Midhurst and Petworth were retained for freight until 12 October 1964 and 23 May 1966 respectively, when the last line to Midhurst was completely abandoned.

A 1985 visit to the area covered in this chapter left vivid impressions of the changes wrought by time. First was the great increase in housing and light industry round the station sites. Bramley and Cranleigh have become towns and the ancient towns of Midhurst and Steyning have outgrown their attractive old centres. Even Rudgwick, Slinfold and Southwater, small villages and hamlets in the 1960s, have expanded out of all recognition. Once again one realised how wrong was that dogmatic assertion in *The Beeching Report* (page 56), 'It has been assumed the pattern [of population and industry] will continue to be basically similar to that which exists at present . . . ' Then there was the rapid growth of the woody vegetation, filling the cuttings at Selham with impenetrable jungle. The eastern portal of Midhurst Tunnel, clearly seen from the road ten years before, was invisible. But the countryside is still beautiful, if the scale is intimate, and well worth visiting.

CHAPTER 6

Minor Holiday Resorts

The long coastline of South Eastern England is nowadays lined with holiday resorts in seemingly unbroken succession as large, old-established and traditional resorts alternate with swollen villages, holiday camps, and caravan sites. Many of the resorts are considerable towns with household names. Brighton is perhaps the most famous of all, but Bognor Regis, Worthing, Eastbourne, Folkestone, Ramsgate and Margate are all well known and these by no means exhaust the list. Some, such as Brighton, Margate and Ramsgate, have their origins prior to the Railway Age; others, such as Eastbourne and Herne Bay only emerged after the coming of the railway. All owed their real growth to the railway.

Success breeds imitation, and there was no lack of speculators hoping to convert small villages into new Brightons in the same way as Brighton itself grew out of Brighthelmstone. They hoped thus to benefit themselves from the seaside holiday habit which grew so rapidly during the Victorian Age. To achieve these ends, it was necessary in the nineteenth century to provide the potential resort with either a railway station on an existing line, or to build a branch from a more remote railway.

Some of these ventures succeeded—Eastbourne and Herne Bay have already been mentioned; Bognor Regis, Bexhill and Westgate were also successful, but there were failures, too. Branch lines were built out to Hayling, Selsey, Littlestone and Allhallows, but development failed to follow until, paradoxically, after the lines were closed.

In the years since 1930, and particularly since 1950,

17. Former LMS Class 2 2–6–2T No 41294 heads the 12.09 from Horsham to Guildford as it takes the branch turnout at Christ's Hospital on 13 March 1965. *(J. Scrace)*

18. A country station scene that is no more. On 10 December 1960 Rudgwick station was still active as part of the Horsham-Guildford service. *(J. S. Gilks)*

Then and now at Henfield
19. A typical LBSC country station about the turn of the century; this was the view looking towards Horsham. *(R. L. Gulliver)*
20. How incredulous the two railwaymen in the picture above would have been had they been told the station would one day be obliterated to make way for 'The Beechings'. The two views were taken from the same spot.

development has indeed taken place, so that the greater part of the coastline has become despoiled by bungalows, huts, chalets, and by caravans. But it was development brought into being to cater for motorised holidaymakers. Although it is true that holidaymakers come for the most part to even the large resorts by car, the railway still has a role to play in serving these towns with their large populations of commuters and retired people, and those visiting London on business or pleasure. There is also a large residual demand for day-trips by rail to those larger resorts.

The small amorphous resorts provide none of these traffics. They provide solely week-end or summer-holiday accommodation for the car-using majority. Even if the rail branches survived into the present era, and some perished even before that, they had no part to play. They were abandoned and have become forgotten. Perhaps the most conspicuous survival of the railway is the occasional coach doing duty as a holiday home.

Allhallows-on-Sea

The first of the abandoned lines we come to is the newest. The Hundred of Hoo is a rather desolate peninsula thrusting out between the Thames and the Medway. It was served by a branch from the North Kent line at Hoo Junction (west of Gravesend) to Port Victoria. This line will be referred to in the next chapter.

The Hundred of Hoo has a core of higher ground on which the villages are located, and which slopes down gently to the grass-covered marshes. These in turn merge into wide mud-flats uncovered at low tide; of beach in the accepted sense of the word there was none. One of the small villages, Hoo Allhallows, lay on higher ground a mile or so from the shore of the Thames estuary. On the slopes between village and shore a land-development company laid out a quite extensive estate and built an hotel.

In June 1929 the Southern Railway obtained a Light Railway Order for a 1¾ mile branch from Stoke Junction on the

Port Victoria line, where a new signal box and loop were provided. The single-track line went into service on 14 May 1932. Coming northward from Stoke Junction, it ran across the marshes to a terminus at Allhallows-on-Sea, an island platform built in the style of the Southern Railway, with a carriage siding, run-round loop and goods siding. A new road was built down to the station by the development company. Allhallows-on-Sea Estates contributed £20,000 to the cost of the line, giving the land where the railway passed through its property. After it had sold out to Aynsley Trust Ltd, the Southern Railway invested in that company.

Most of the Port Victoria trains were diverted to Allhallows, leaving the latter with only two a day for workers. The new branch had about six services a day; two up trains in the morning and two down in the evening were provided with through coaches to and from London, attached to and detached from North Kent trains at Gravesend.

Attempts to sell housing plots failed completely, and the through coaches were withdrawn at the end of the 1932 summer. Day-trips proved quite popular, though precisely what happened on a wet day one shudders to think. The author remembers booking a few intrepid excursionists to Allhallows at Charlton on the North Kent line on August Bank Holiday 1938, the train comprising an ex-SECR 'long-set' of eight non-corridor coaches, hauled by a C class 0–6–0. Optimistically, the SR doubled the branch in 1935.

Most of the local services were provided by pull-and-push trains hauled by H class 0–4–4Ts, but in the last year or two of working a class 33 diesel locomotive and a one-coach train was sometimes used. Traffic, however, fell away; the line was singled again in 1957, the last passenger train ran on 3 December 1961, and the line abandoned after less than thirty years.

There has been considerable post-war development at Allhallows, especially since 1960. The station building survived as a store in connection with the caravan site which covers the former station yard. Nearby the hotel, the 'British Pilot', and a surprising block of flats, Albany Court, are all that remain of the hopes and expectations of the Southern Railway and of the Allhallows-on-Sea Estate company.

The Sheppey Light Railway

The Isle of Sheppey, east of the Medway estuary, is geologically and scenically very similiar to the Hundred of Hoo peninsula, but is completely separated from the mainland by the channel of the Swale. However, it has what the Hundred of Hoo lacks, a sizeable town of nearly 15,000 inhabitants. Sheerness, in the north-western extremity of the island, grew up around the former naval base, which is now a commercial port dealing with LASH (Lighter Aboard Ship) vessels. There are also a glass works and a steel plant.

Sheerness was reached by a seven-mile single-track branch from Sittingbourne, which opened on 19 July 1860. It was electrified in 1959 as part of the Phase I of the Kent Coast programme and doubled as far as the Kingsferry Bridge. It has a considerable passenger and freight traffic, but runs along the west coast of Sheppey, thus leaving most of the island remote from a railway. The possibility of traffic was limited as the area was very sparsely peopled. Advantage was taken of the 1896 Light Railway Act to promote a line 8¾ miles long from Queenborough on the Sheerness branch to Leysdown. On 3 April 1899 an Order was granted for the construction by an independent company, the Sheppey Light Railway.

The line was opened on 1 August 1901. It was built by Colonel Stephens and bore all the hallmarks of his handiwork, purely a surface line without earthworks. Although the highest point was only 100ft above sea level, gradients were heavy, with inclines of 1 in 70, 1 in 80 and 1 in 100. There were no bridges and eight level crossings over public roads; there were no gates on some, while at others the gates were operated by the train guards. There were no signals, except at the termini and at Eastchurch, the only passing loop.

Trains were controlled by staff and ticket. The stations were primitive; H. A. Vallance, writing in 1934, said that some were rebuilt with corrugated iron waiting-rooms, 'a great improvement'! There was an overall speed limit of 25mph and one of 10mph approaching the ungated crossings.

The Sheppey Light was always worked by the SECR and in 1905 it was absorbed by the LCDR. This was because the SECR was only a managing committee of the two companies. The two latter remained in existence as legal entities and continued as owners of their respective lines.

The passenger service was meagre. In 1930 there were six round trips by a pull-and-push train, with a late working on Wednesdays. By 1948 these had been reduced to four. There never was much freight. In 1937 this was catered for by one trip to Sheerness East and two to Eastchurch. Leysdown traffic went by the 16.04 mixed from Queenborough, which returned as a mixed working as far as Eastchurch. All traffic ceased on 4 December 1950.

The up platform at Queenborough was an island and trains for Leysdown left from the outer face. There was no direct connection with the 'main line' and the branch had independent run-round facilities. The line bore north-east across the marshes and at 1½ miles, where the main road to Sheerness was crossed, Sheerness East was located. As with all the stations and halts, Sheerness East had a single short platform and primitive accommodation. There was also a siding. Sheerness was the better part of a mile away, but though there was some local development, to use the train would have been most inconvenient.

The line then turned eastward and where the main road to Leysdown was crossed East Minster-on-Sea was located (2½ miles). The line then climbed steeply at 1 in 70 to an ungated crossing, beyond which Minster-on-Sea (3⅛ miles) was situated, a single platform with a corrugated-iron booking office on the north side of the track, and a siding on the south. An extensive building development was laid out between the railway and the sea to the north. It was never really successful, but during the 1920s and 1930s a sporadic rash of wooden and brick bungalows, huts and old railway carriages extended over the low clay plateau.

The line ran steeply down past Brambledown Halt (four miles) and Grove Siding (five miles) to Eastchurch Station (5½ miles). To the south was one of the earliest military flying establishments, dating from before World War I. The site is now occupied by an open prison, but in its heyday it brought much traffic to the line and freight traffic was dealt with here and at Grove. There was a private siding to the airfield at Eastchurch. A mile beyond Eastchurch was Holford Siding. Beyond that was Harty Road Halt (seven miles) where the Leysdown Road was again crossed, but otherwise the halt was virtually nowhere from the traffic viewpoint. The line now paralleled the road into Leysdown (8¾ miles). The terminus was a simple one; a platform, run-round loop and siding. At Leysdown, and at the neighbouring Warden on higher ground to the north estates were laid out, but development was very slow until after 1945. In any case it came too late to have benefitted the railway.

The Inspecting Officer's report on a collision between a private car and a train on the ungated crossing at Minster on 26 April 1935 throws some light on operating methods. The whole line was in the charge of the Queenborough station master. Of the seven stations, three were unmanned and four manned by only a single porter. The train concerned was the 18.55 from Queenborough and the porter at Minster had gone off duty. Although owned by a main line company, the atmosphere of the Sheppey Light was more akin to a Colonel Stephens line.

Because earthworks were few and the stations were such simple affairs there are few traces of the line left. Development has continued rapidly since the line was closed and a lot of it is built over. Housing extends all the way from Queenborough to Minster alongside the old line. Leysdown has also expanded in a caravan and holiday camp way. The former station yard is now a car and coach park.

Sandgate

The SER main line approached Folkestone running under the chalk scarp of the North Downs, well inland from the coast which here runs almost parallel with the scarp. It thus missed Hythe, which was served by buses and coaches connecting with trains at Westenhanger station. Hythe was one of the Cinque Ports and until the building of Folkestone Harbour and the coming of the railway it was more important than Folkestone. It was a market town, military centre and resort. Between it and Folkestone in the latter part of the nineteenth century estates were laid out on the seashore at Seabrook and Sandgate.

The SER promoted a branch in 1864 to serve the three resorts and this was opened on 9 October 1874. It was 3½ miles long and double-tracked, leaving the main line at a junction 1¼ miles east of Westenhanger. Branch trains connected with main line services at the latter until Sandling Junction station was opened at the junction in 1888. In 1876 powers were obtained to extend the branch along the seashore to Folkestone Harbour, in order to by-pass the existing Folkestone Harbour branch with its awkward junction and steep grade. The line was never built, however.

Sandling Junction had two platforms on the main line and two on the branch. The line ran down past Saltwood Castle to Hythe station (1½ miles) and then under the cliffs past Seabrook to Sandgate (3½ miles). Neither station was conveniently sited, especially Hythe, which was up a long and steeply-inclined station road. There was a horse tram along the shore road, but branches to the stations came to nothing.

Traffic on the branch always was light. It was more convenient to patronise the main line stations at Shorncliffe and Folkestone. The section beyond Hythe was closed from 1 April 1931. The East Kent Road Car Company built a garage on part of the site of Sandgate. For many years that part of the station reserved for the use of Gentlemen survived for the benefit of the bus crews, and in 1974 it was still recognisable though completely derelict. The branch was closed altogether in 1943 and re-opened in 1945 to Hythe with two trains a day. This was no way to build up traffic and final closure was effected on 3 December 1951. A local independent bus operator put on a connecting service from Sandling for Hythe, the new name of Sandling Junction, to all parts of Hythe.

Sandgate station was approached on a high embankment. Pre-1939 houses and bungalows were erected on this, perched uneasily atop it, with excessively steep front and back gardens. In 1974 new houses were being built on and around Hythe station, but bulldozers were obliterating all traces of the line.

Dungeness and New Romney

South of Hythe lies the extensive Romney Marsh, flat, and only a few feet above sea level. The coastline of the marsh thrusts out into the Channel the shingle banks of Dungeness. The shore shelves very steeply and large ships can approach close in, where they pick up pilots for passing through the Straits of Dover.

The Ashford–Hastings line was opened by the SER in 1851. It crossed the marsh from Ham Street to Rye. In 1873 the Rye & Dungeness Railway and Pier Company was incorporated to build a branch from the Ashford–Hastings line to Dungeness. Neither railway nor pier was built, though the powers passed to the SER in 1875 (page 123). Later a nominally-independent Lydd Railway Company (absorbed by the SER in 1895) was floated to build a line from Appledore through Lydd to Dungeness. On 7 December 1881 the line was opened throughout for freight traffic and to Lydd for passengers. Passenger traffic to Dungeness began on 1 April 1883. In 1882 powers were obtained for a branch to New Romney, opened on 19 June 1884.

Appledore station stands isolated, apart from an adjacent inn, lost in the expanse of Romney Marsh 1½ miles from the village whose name it bears. The author can remember once, having dallied too long in Appledore, running along the endless road under a hot afternoon sun, spurred on by the view of the train from Rye, to reach the station breathless and exhausted just too late as the Ashford-bound H-tank clanked away over the level-crossing. He then had plenty of opportunity to contemplate Appledore station.

Appledore is an ordinary two-platform station, and beyond the former goods yard the single track branch curves away across the dead-level of the marsh to reach Brookland Halt (2½ miles). Originally there were two platforms and a passing loop, but the latter was taken up in 1920. Lydd (seven miles) was the next station, serving the tranquil town with its wide main street and ancient church. In 1974 it still survived with a loop, two platforms and quite a big goods yard. There was connection with the six-mile Lydd Military Railway (1883–c1926) which ran to the artillery range.

A mile beyond Lydd was the junction for the New Romney branch. There was no signal box or passing loop, just a single set of points worked by a ground frame unlocked by the train staff and operated by the guard. The branch ended at the single platform at Dungeness (10¾ miles), hard by the lighthouse and the Romney Hythe & Dymchurch Light Railway station of later years. Passenger traffic was extremely meagre; the author sometimes speculates on who caught the 22.20 (SO) from Dungeness to Ashford on a winter's night. Shingle provided some traffic, including flints for the Potteries to provide glaze on the china.

The New Romney branch was three miles long, and ended in a small two-platformed terminus with a small goods yard. In 1927 one of the sidings was extended across the road to serve the RHDR depot. New Romney & Littlestone-on-Sea station lay equidistant from the ancient Cinque Port and the small resort of Littlestone-on-Sea. Here subsequent to the opening of the railway a tall, gaunt Victorian terrace of boarding houses was built together with an hotel, but as a resort it did not get going until the rash of seaside bungalows spread down the coast in the 1920s and 1930s.

The two branches were served by the same train. In some

cases the train from Appledore went either to the one or the other terminus. In others the New Romney passengers were decanted at Lydd, while the train went on to Dungeness, taking with it the Lydd stationmaster to sell tickets to any aspiring passengers. The train would return to Lydd, drop its passengers, pick up the New Romney contingent and set off.

In the 1920s seaside development proceeded apace. The Southern realigned the New Romney branch nearer the coast. The junction was re-located $1\frac{1}{4}$ miles further on, leaving only a $1\frac{1}{2}$ mile stub. The old line was rejoined $\frac{3}{4}$ mile from New Romney. Two new stations were provided at Lydd-on-Sea ($10\frac{3}{4}$ miles from Appledore) and Greatstone (fourteen miles), the former having a passing loop. The diversion came into use on 4 July 1937, and at the same time Dungeness was closed to passengers. Shingle was sent from Dungeness until May 1953.

The train service was never lavish, but got better as the years went by. In 1905 there were eight weekday departures from Appledore, four serving both termini, and four New Romney only. There was a single Sunday departure for New Romney. This pattern was almost unchanged in 1925. By 1952 there was a definite increase with nine trains from Appledore to New Romney with two coming through from Ashford, and four trains on Sundays, all from Ashford.

In addition on summer Saturdays the 11.30 and 14.15 services from Charing Cross ran through to New Romney. The former consisted of nine modern corridor coaches, by far the heaviest train venturing down the branch regularly. The 14.15 was diagrammed to have five corridors for Folkestone Junction. The rear five, a three-set and two 'swingers', as the Southern men called single coaches not marshalled in sets, were detached at Ashford and worked forward to New Romney. Southern stock working was never simple—that was its fascination—and the return services did not balance. The stock of the 11.30 returned at 14.28. But of the 14.15, the corridor set and one 'swinger' went to Ashford as the 16.55 stopping train. A three-corridor set came down from Ashford as the 05.50 passenger to form the 11.23 for Charing Cross.

The carriage working notice is silent about the fate of the second 'swinger'—one has a momentary fantasy of the New Romney yard gradually filling up with odd corridor coaches as the summer advanced.

After electrification to Dover in 1962 and the prohibition of steam on the South Eastern, the diesel-electric sets, usually three-car, sometimes the six-car units, took over completely. There were nine departures from Ashford and two from Appledore, but the through Saturday trains from Charing Cross ceased.

The New Romney branch was listed for closure in the Beeching Report of 1963, along with the Ashford–Hastings line. The closure ritual dragged out a long time. Bus services always were a very poor substitute. Closure to passengers and public freight finally came on 6 March 1967, the line being retained as a siding to milepost 74, which is in fact the site of the newer junction with the new Romney branch. Two short sidings along each right-of-way are retained to load the containers of atomic waste from the two atomic power stations. Aggregate is also loaded at a new siding at milepost 73. In 1974 six trains were being despatched daily to Chislehurst, Allington, Merstham and Gatwick. This traffic still passes so the branch sees more daily freight traffic than ever.

The author's last sight of a steam train on the New Romney branch was on 25 February 1962. It was a bitter grey day as two old SECR veterans, an H class 0–4–4T and a C class 0–6–0 hauled the railtour train 'Kentish Venturer' out of New Romney across the marsh to Appledore, where Schools class 30926 *Repton* was waiting. The next day steam locomotives were to be banned from the South Eastern Division. But even today both the old and the new tracks can be traced across the shingle banks of Dungeness.

By all accounts the Ashford–Hastings line should have figured in this volume, but the trains are still running though at reduced speeds because of the bad state of the track. Substitute buses could not be licensed before road improvements were made. Local authorities and many residents campaigned for the line to be retained, and even British

Rail wanted to be let off the self-imposed hook of closure. On 31 July 1974 the Minister of Transport announced that the line was one of those being considered for closure on which services would continue indefinitely.

Crowhurst and Bexhill West

In 1850 there was no settlement of any size or importance anywhere along the coast between the small ports of Newhaven and Hastings but after the coming of the railway, Eastbourne, Bexhill and St Leonards grew steadily. All of them were deliberately planned in their early period, but straggled more haphazardly in later years along the coast and inland. All the resorts between Brighton and Hastings were served by the LBSCR while St Leonards and Hastings were also reached by the SER. The latter supported the Crowhurst, Sidley & Bexhill Railway Company, incorporated to build a $4\frac{1}{2}$ mile branch from the Tonbridge–Hastings line at Crowhurst. The line was opened on 1 June 1902. Worked by the SECR, it was absorbed by the SER in 1905.

The branch was laid out in a style which was unusually spacious for the SER and its creatures. Crowhurst was a new station. The two through platforms were served by loops off the main lines, and there was a bay at the country end of each. Crowhurst comprised little more than a church and inn, but in later years there was some housing development along the long private road to the station.

The double-tracked branch bore off to the south, curving down to the seventeen-arch Combe Haven brick viaduct across the Crowhurst Valley, the principal engineering feature of the branch, whose maximum height was 70ft. The line descended to the only intermediate station, Sidley ($3\frac{5}{8}$ miles), which served an inland suburb of Bexhill.

Bexhill, renamed Bexhill West by the SR, was enormous. A large concourse gave access to a long two-faced platform, with room for another. There was a large goods depot and extensive sidings. The front of the station was separated from the LBSCR only by the width of a road, but it was halfway between Bexhill Central and Collington Halt.

Bexhill West was sixty-two miles from Charing Cross, while Bexhill Central was 71¾ from Victoria (seventy-eight via Eastbourne). The SECR, and after it the Southern Railway, ran through portions, and even through trains. In 1925 there were eighteen weekday departures from Crowhurst, but electrification of the former LBSCR line in 1935 swung the balance and traffic declined thereafter. The last through service was withdrawn in 1940. The branch pull-and-push train connected with almost every main line train at Crowhurst. There was one freight train a day. There was also an unadvertised school train from Etchingham at 08.11, returning from Bexhill West at 16.26. It was made up of a pull-and-push set and a 100 seat non-corridor coach. Later, a six-car diesel-electric unit was provided.

Between 27 November 1949 and 5 June 1950 Bo Peep Tunnel, between West St Leonards and Warrior Square, was closed for repairs and all Hastings trains were diverted to Bexhill West. Connecting buses from Hastings navigated dangerously the narrow roads to Crowhurst. On 9 June 1958 diesel-electric multiple units took over until total closure on 15 June 1964.

Hayling Island

Sir John Betjeman once described Hayling as 'just a piece of inland Hampshire that has slithered—oaks, elms, winding lanes and all—out of England into the sea'. He divides Hayling life into three, farming, amateur sailing, and seaside holiday camps. The two last at least are booming activities, but the boom had nothing to do with the railway, although it survived into the yacht and caravan age. Hayling has been a minor resort since the eighteenth century. In 1824 a narrow wooden toll bridge at Langstone replaced an erratic ferry. Its successor is still subject to extreme congestion.

The LBSCR arrived at Havant in 1847, and the LSWR in 1859. Efforts were made by local businessmen to provide the island with rail connection. On 23 July 1860 the Hayling Railways Company was incorporated. The intention was to build the line on an embankment off the west coast of the island so that some 1,000 acres of land thus enclosed could be reclaimed. Work began in 1863, but ran into difficulties, the sea constantly washing away the half-built embankment. An Act of 1864 authorised a $1\frac{1}{4}$ mile extension to a pier and docks at South Hayling, but it failed to infuse new capital into the scheme. Not until January 1865 was the first mile to Langstone opened for freight, though Langstone Quay was then a busy port bringing much traffic.

Francis Fuller, a London businessman, then intervened. Impressed by the natural charm of the island, he purchased building land at Hayling, and brought new life to the railway. The diversion of the line on to the Island itself was also authorised, somewhat belatedly, by an Act of 12 August 1867.

The line was actually opened to public traffic on 8 July 1867. It was worked by the contractors with an 0–4–2T and some four-wheeled coaches hired from the LSWR. The LBSCR took over operations in January 1872, the temporary arrangements being converted to a long lease in 1874. The Hayling Company itself was finally absorbed in 1923, technically after the creation of the Southern Railway, but prior to the final dissolution of the Brighton company.

The Hayling Island trains left from a short bay at the east end of the up platform at Havant. Beyond the station yard the single-track bore sharply away to the south to reach Langston (*sic*) (one mile), a simple wooden platform and hut. At one time there was a short branch to Langstone (*sic*) Quay.

Hayling Island lies between Langstone Harbour and Chichester Harbour. The broad channel connecting them is crossed by the road bridge. The railway paralleled the road on the west, crossing on to the island by an embankment and a wooden viaduct with an opening span. It was this viaduct which limited the locomotives which could be used to the A1X 0–6–0T, the famous Terriers.

Another simple halt was provided at North Hayling (nearly

2½ miles). The terminus (4½ miles), originally South Hayling, but renamed Hayling Island in 1892, was more substantial. Brick-built offices were provided on the single platform with a short bay, and there were run-round facilities and a small goods yard. No intermediate passing places were provided, trains being controlled by staff-and-ticket.

In later years the Terriers were allowed to take three corridor coaches, four if the service was non-stop, which dwarfed the tiny locomotives. Summer traffic was heavy to the end, but the winter service was very lightly patronised and a single coach sufficed. In 1961 32,176 tickets were collected at Hayling Island during August (over 1,000 per working day), but only 2,077 during March (only 80 per working day). On one Sunday almost 7,000 visitors to the Island were carried; the trains would have been as well filled as a Dartford Loop train at the peak hour.

The Working Timetable of 2 July 1939 showed seventeen departures on weekdays, with an extra on Wednesdays. The 07.20 and 09.17 were mixed trains. On summer Saturdays there were twenty-four departures and for much of the day the service was on an interval basis. Trains left at 23 minutes past the hour for Hayling Island, taking only ten minutes, and at 50 minutes past the hour calling at the two halts and taking thirteen minutes. There were twenty-two departures on summer Sundays.

By 1961 steam on the Southern was doomed. Modernisation would be impossible unless the viaduct were rebuilt. The line was closed completely on 4 November 1963 and the 'Hayling Billy' became only a memory. The name is, however, preserved by the public house near St Mary's church, South Hayling, where for a time Terrier No. 46 *Newington,* in full though weatherbeaten LBSCR livery, stood duty as the inn sign. The Hayling was one of those friendly intimate lines. Sam Waldron, one of the guards, knew many passengers by name and would delay the departure of the last train until all his regulars were aboard, going outside the station to urge on latecomers.

CHAPTER 7

Casualties of the Feud

Competition between rival companies was a feature of the Victorian railway scene. This could take a number of forms, which were controlled with greater or less severity by Parliament: the building of 'blocking' lines by one company to prevent the entry of other companies into an area it regarded as its own, duplication of lines between common points, indulging in rate wars and, rather too infrequently, the introduction of better services and faster trains of more comfortable stock.

The mutual enmity of the SER and the LBSCR has been referred to at some length in Chapter 4, with the latter building 'blocking' lines in the Weald to prevent the SER from reaching Brighton or Eastbourne. In turn, there was also little love lost between the LBSCR and the LSWR where their interests clashed, as at Portsmouth.

The internecine warfare between the SER and the LCDR was fought on an even more vicious level, which resulted in the mutual impoverishment of the two companies without any particular benefit to the people of Kent in terms of cheaper and better train services. One of the results was not only the building of 'blocking' lines, but the lavish provision of duplicate facilities not only in London but between London and many Kentish towns.

Obviously, several of the forgotten lines were casualties of the 'Feud', as the struggle between the two companies came to be known, in that they became redundant after peace finally settled over the Kentish battlefield with the so-called 'Fusion' of 1899. It is surprising how few these casualties have been, and how many duplicate lines have survived as a necessary part of the railway system to deal with the constant increase in traffic resulting from economic and social development in Kent. Nothing approaching a main line has yet been closed, unlike the extensive closures of duplicate facilities in West Yorkshire, South Wales and the West Midlands or the elimination of the former Great Central London Extension.

The Feud

Before describing the casualties, it is worthwhile briefly summarising the history of the Feud, for the geography of the Kentish railway system cannot be understood without an understanding of the course the Feud took.

In 1853 the SER reached, albeit by roundabout routes, all the places in Kent of any importance, except Sittingbourne and Faversham. Its reputation also stood high, which would have seemed incredible twenty years later. But in that year the seeds of trouble were sown when the East Kent Railway was incorporated to extend the North Kent line of the SER from Strood to Canterbury.

The SER regarded the East Kent as a satellite, but failed to absorb the small company and, to cut a long story short, the East Kent was extended westward to join a series of railways connecting St Mary Cray with Victoria, and eastward from Canterbury to Dover. In 1859 it blossomed into the London Chatham & Dover Railway, and by 1861 a rival route to that of the SER was available throughout between London and Dover via Chatham. The situation was potentially explosive. The continental traffic was the most important single source of revenue for both the SER and the LCDR, while the two companies were also rivals for the Medway Towns and Canterbury traffic. It was made worse by the personal rivalry between the two men in charge of the companies, Sir Edward Watkin and J. S. Forbes.

Edward Watkin was born in 1819, the son of a Manchester businessman. He joined the Trent Valley Railway as secretary,

The Midhurst Line
21. Ex-LBSC 0-6-0, BR No 32526, heading the daily Horsham-Midhurst freight, diverges from the main line at Hardham Junction on 20 August 1957.
22. After it arrived at Midhurst No 32526 made a trip to the brickworks sidings. It returned past the abandoned LSW station on its way back to the LBSC goods yard.

23. A resort that failed in railway days: Albany Court was built next to the new station of Allhallows-on-Sea but the development ceased for a quarter century.
24. The line through Groombridge had the melancholy distinction of being the first in SE England to be closed to passengers (in 1985) since Lewes–Uckfield closed in 1969. In 1958 a Brighton–Tunbridge Wells train arrives behind a U1 Class Mogul, while a train for Brighton awaits departure.

later transferring to the LNWR then under the ruthless direction of Captain Huish. In 1854 he became general manager of the Manchester, Sheffield & Lincolnshire and chairman ten years later. In the same year he was invited to join the SER board, and was elected chairman in 1866. Among his other offices were a directorship of the Channel Tunnel Company and, from 1872, chairman of the Metropolitan Railway. James Staats Forbes was born in Aberdeen in 1823. He joined the Great Western Railway and later managed the British-owned Dutch Rhenish Railway. In 1861 he was appointed general manager of the LCDR, but did not become chairman until 1873. A year before, he was made chairman of the Metropolitan District Railway. The two men were bitter personal rivals, carrying their animosities from the fields of Kent to the tunnels below the London streets. It is also widely held that it was Forbes who influenced the War Office to oppose the Channel Tunnel.

But alongside this story of rivalry is the underlying current setting towards the eventual and inevitable fusion of the two companies, long delayed by the rivalry between Watkin and Forbes. The first manifestation was the Continental Agreement of 1865 even if, like the 1848 Agreement between the SER and LBSCR, it also formed the basis of later trouble.

The definitive 1865 Agreement repeated the terms of a provisional one drawn up two years earlier. All continental traffic between London and any port between Hastings and Margate inclusive, and all local traffic between London and both Folkestone and Dover was to be pooled. Initially the LCDR share was to be 32 per cent, but this share was to be gradually increased until parity was reached in 1874. The effect of the pooling was virtually nullified by another clause permitting either company to make a claim for an allowance to cover working expenses, should it carry in any one year a greater proportion of the total traffic than its stipulated proportion of the gross receipts. It was this clause which was the basis of subsequent competition, while the geographical limits of the agreement also led to trouble.

The financial structure of the LCDR was rickety in the extreme and dubious extensions of the system led to further over-capitalisation. In the year 1866 financial crisis affected many railway companies. We saw some of the consequences on the LBSCR in Chapter 4. The Chatham was reduced to bankruptcy when in that year blocks of debentures paid to contractors in lieu of cash fell due and there was no means of meeting the obligations. Forbes was appointed one of the receivers, and in 1867 and 1869 Arrangement Acts were passed granting special powers to raise capital and granting moritoria on debts. Under Forbes' management the Chatham regained solvency, but it never paid a dividend on the ordinary stock.

The SER avoided bankruptcy, but its resources were over-stretched by the rivalry, and prosperity eluded it. The train services of both companies stagnated and there was no money to renew the antiquated rolling stock. In fairness, however, the LCDR was early in the field of vital safety measures: absolute block working and continuous brakes on passenger trains.

From 1868 onwards a number of amalgamation schemes were canvassed, with or without LBSCR participation, but all foundered. After 1890 some progress was made, especially after 1894 when Watkin retired through ill-health. In that year an Act was obtained to permit the LCDR to negotiate with the SER on all traffic not covered by the 1865 Agreement. In addition the fortunes of the LCDR were rising compared with those of the SER, though it would be unable to raise new capital. The LCDR could now obtain better terms, and the SER was more ready to agree. The two companies began a working union on 1 January 1899, retrospectively authorised by the Act of 1 August of that year. Under the terms of the Act the two companies retained their separate entities, capital structure and legal ownership of their track. For operating and commercial purposes the two systems were managed as one by the South Eastern & Chatham Railway Companies Managing Committee. Staff and rolling stock were pooled, as were the traffic receipts.

The Main Lines

The LCDR line from Victoria to Dover via Crystal Palace and Chatham, opened in 1861, was 82½ miles, against the SER's 87¼ miles from London Bridge to Dover via Redhill. This led the latter to build its Sevenoaks cut-off, opened in 1868. After the LCDR opened its Penge route, the distance from Victoria via Chatham and from Charing Cross via Tonbridge was virtually equal at 77¼ miles.

At the London end, the SER opened its extension to Cannon Street and Charing Cross, dating from 1864 and 1866 respectively. The LCDR replied with its 'City Line' through Ludgate Hill to the Metropolitan Widened Lines and Farringdon, opened throughout in 1866. Holborn Viaduct dates from 1874.

At the eastern end of its line, the LCDR reached Margate and Ramsgate in 1864 by a branch from Faversham. It also promoted piecemeal yet another route to Dover from Swanley Junction to Ashford via Maidstone, which was completed in 1884.

These lines still form the backbone of the Southern Region in Kent, and with their heavy passenger and increasing freight traffic are anything but forgotten. It is now time to review the casualties of the 'Feud', in the remainder of this chapter and in the next. In addition, some attention will be paid to forgotten train services.

The Thanet Lines

The SER reached Ramsgate in 1846 by a branch from Ashford down the Stour Valley through Canterbury to the estuarine marshes at Minster. From there it climbed steeply on to the low plateau of the Isle of Thanet to reach a terminus at Ramsgate Town, located on the edge of the built-up area. It had two low and rather short platforms with four tracks between them. In later years a very short, narrow and low platform was provided between the two inside tracks. It was an inconvenient station, but enlargement was difficult as the line to Margate branched off at the very platform ends. In 1863 a spur was provided to allow through running to Margate. The next year a station called St Lawrence was opened at the bridge just west of the spur. It was closed in 1916.

The Margate branch was 3¾ miles long and without intermediate stations. It ran almost dead straight and level across the chalk plateau to terminate conveniently on the sea-front just west of the town. A temporary wooden station was used until the permanent station was ready in 1858. Platforms were also provided to serve the Tivoli Pleasure Gardens (now Tivoli Park) where the Southern's goods station later stood.

The LCDR route to Thanet was originally planned under the Margate Railway Act of 1859 to terminate at Margate, rather more inconveniently than the SER at the top end of the present station approach, approximately on the site of the parcels platform. Before completion of the line, the extension to Ramsgate was authorised by the Kent Coast Railway Act of 1861. This necessitated a new alignment, curving sharply eastward just short of the planned site. The station, opened in 1863, stood on the site of the present station. Just to the east the line crossed over the SER line. For some reason, the LCDR decided on a second station, a terminal adjoining the SER station to the east—and reached by a spur facing Ramsgate! The spur was completed in 1864, retrospective powers being obtained in 1865. It was never used as a station, being let to the caterers Spiers & Ponds who called it 'Hall by the sea'. In 1919 it became part of 'Dreamland' all traces being obliterated when the present amusement park was laid out in the 1930s.

Half a mile east of Margate, a station called East Margate was provided at an inconvenient inland site. The line now struck across interior Thanet, up 1 in 88 to Broadstairs, and then down at 1 in 75 through a cutting and a 1,638yd tunnel to emerge into the platforms of Ramsgate and St Lawrence-on-Sea station, located on the very foreshore close by the

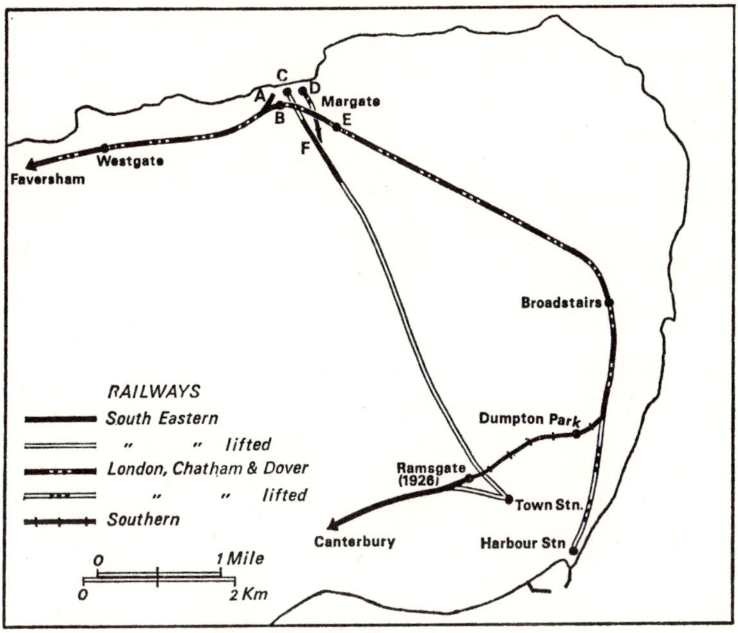

The Thanet lines in 1974

Key to stations at Margate

A Original LCD terminus
B Margate (originally Margate West)
C Margate Sands SER
D 'Hall by the Sea'
E Margate East
F Goods Depot (Tivoli platform)

harbour. Though the LCDR had powers for a horse tramway to the quays, these were never rail-connected. The station had two long platforms with a short bay in each. There were three tracks between the main platforms and a short length of overall roof.

After fusion there was some rationalisation of station names. In June 1899 the LCDR station at Margate became Margate West, and East Margate became Margate East. The SER station became Margate Sands. At Ramsgate, the SER and LCDR stations became Ramsgate Town and Ramsgate Harbour respectively. The SECR also planned rationalisation of the lines, but World War I came and it was left to the Southern Railway to bring the plan to fruition.

Back at Minster, a branch through Sandwich to Deal had

been opened in 1847. In 1881, as a result of one of the rare periods of cooperation between SER and LCDR, the Dover and Deal Joint Line was built. As part of this scheme, a little-used spur was laid in at Minster to allow through running from Deal to Ramsgate Town.

The services to Thanet were quite separate. The SER ran through services from London via Canterbury to Margate Sands, reversing at Ramsgate Town and with connections at Minster for Deal. The LCDR ran via Margate West to Ramsgate Harbour. This pattern was left unchanged by the SECR and the SR until the new works were completed in 1926.

These works consisted basically of a new line $1\frac{3}{8}$ miles long, connecting the SER line half a mile west of Ramsgate Town with the LCDR line in the chalk cutting at the northern portal of the tunnel up from the harbour. This allowed the Town and Harbour stations to be closed, the traffic being concentrated on the present Ramsgate station, unfortunately rather remotely situated. At the other end, Margate West was completely rebuilt and greatly enlarged. Margate Sands and the branch from Ramsgate was abandoned. Finally a new and better-aligned spur was provided at Minster from the Deal direction.

The services via Chatham now terminated at the new Ramsgate. The services via Ashford were directed through Dover and Deal. While some terminated at Ramsgate, many ran through to Margate. Connections were provided at Ashford for Canterbury, Ramsgate and Margate. Since electrification, trains have been divided at Ashford to reach Ramsgate via Canterbury and via Deal.

There are almost no traces of Ramsgate Town, except for a portion of wall. The approach has been built over, but the alignment of the streets reveals its general direction. Ramsgate Harbour is now an amusement park. The tunnel was used (1936–65) for part of its length by a 2ft gauge electric railway. Margate Sands became a café and survived, recognisable as a former station, until 1961. The approach line is easily traceable across the open country from Ramsgate. At the Margate end a large goods depot, part of the 1926 rationalisation, was built along the formation, together with a new spur from the main line east of the passenger station. It closed, and is now a coach park and industrial estate

The Elham Valley

In 1863 the SER opened two stations to the west of Folkestone Junction, its main station in that town. These were named Cheriton Arch and Shorncliffe & Sandgate. As Lord Radnor developed his estate in the high ground west of the valley in which the old fishing village was located, Cheriton Arch was renamed Radnor Park in 1886 and Folkestone Central, by then an appropriate title, in 1896. The other was renamed Shorncliffe Camp in 1874. In 1881 the SER replaced the rickety wooden station there with a new and enlarged brick-built structure 150yd to the east.

The SER now contended that these two stations 'were not Folkestone' and withheld its receipts from the pool set up by the 1865 Agreement. Shorncliffe Camp was also provided with a better service and lower fares than the other two Folkestone stations. In 1887 the LCDR initiated legal proceedings to recover its share of the receipts. Although judgement was eventually given in its favour, the litigation was prolonged and costly. The LCDR was awarded £85,000, but its costs were estimated at £250,000. Incidentally, Shorncliffe Camp became Shorncliffe in 1926, and Folkestone West in 1961. In the latter year Folkestone Junction then became Folkestone East and was closed to passengers in 1965.

As part of the struggle over the Folkestone receipts the LCDR sought powers in 1883 to reach Folkestone by a branch from Kearsney on its main line between Canterbury and Dover. The branch was to run up the Alkham Valley and presumably tunnel under the crest of the Downs.

The LCDR Bill was rejected, but to counter further moves by that Company, the SER took over in 1884 the Elham Valley Light Railway Company. This had been incorporated in 1881, taking advantage of the Railway Facilities Act of 1870 (p 31), to build a line from Folkestone to Canterbury. Trouble over the Elham Valley had started in 1864 when the Elham Valley Railway had been incorporated. Connection at Canterbury could have been with either the SER or LCDR, and the former was apprehensive the EVR would offer itself to the Chatham, but the latter's bankruptcy in 1866 caused the plans to fall into abeyance for fifteen years. The Elham Valley Railway was certainly regarded by the SER as a 'blocking' line.

The Elham Valley was 16·88 miles long, running from Cheriton Junction on the main line from Ashford to Dover, 1⅛ miles west of Shorncliffe (Folkestone West) to Harbledown Junction on the Ashford–Ramsgate line, ⁴/₅ mile south of Canterbury West. It was opened as far as Barham on 4 July 1887, and on to Harbledown Junction on 1 July 1889. The independent company had been absorbed by the SER in 1884.

The Elham Valley diverged at Cheriton Junction, but there was a third line from Shorncliffe used by the branch trains in both directions. Cheriton Halt (opened 1908), which was located ⅝ mile east of the Junction, had only a single platform on this line, so only branch trains could call. When the main line was electrified in 1962, the associated improvements included quadrupling from the site of Cheriton Junction to just east of Folkestone Central. The Elham Valley line became the down slow; Folkestone West was rebuilt with two platforms on the slow lines, and Folkestone Central with two island platforms.

The Elham Valley line bore northward, climbing steeply towards the North Downs scarp. This was crossed by the deep and narrow Etchinghill Gap which leads into the Elham Valley itself. The throat of the gap (negotiated by a tunnel) is over 350ft, 150ft higher than Cheriton Junction. Lyminge, 4⅜ miles from Shorncliffe, is the highest valley village. The station was conveniently situated, just off the High Street.

The Elham Valley is a picturesque chalk valley. It is deep

and narrow and there is not much room for the river, the Nail Bourne, the B2065 and the track of the old railway. One of the attractions of the valley is the line of villages and hamlets. One such is Ottinge, where 4/5 mile beyond Lyminge a public siding was provided at an overbridge crossed by a side road. Almost two miles from Lyminge was the next station, Elham, conveniently situated for the village. Another public siding was provided at Wingmore (1½ miles from Elham). Both sidings faced Cheriton, and were served by southbound trains.

The next station was Barham, just over four miles from Elham. In such a narrow valley the station sites had to be convenient, provided the line kept to the floor of the valley. North of Barham the line began to climb the valley side. There were no facilities at Kingston village, and the station at Bishopsbourne (2¼ miles from Barham) was up a steep hill. At Bridge, the Nail Bourne swings north and the line bears away from the valley. Bridge station (1⅜ miles from Bishopsbourne) was high above and remote from the large village, which was on the A2, and buses early robbed the station of its traffic.

The line climbed over the orchard-crowned ridge and dropped down the side of the Stour Valley to Harbledown Junction. Canterbury South station was 1⅞ miles from Bridge. During the 1930s building development reached out to it, but whoever used it is questionable as it would have been quicker to have walked into the city. Harbledown Junction was located immediately on the Ashford side of the LCDR overbridge.

Originally double-track, it was temporarily singled in World War I. Final singling took place north of Lyminge in 1931. There were no passing places. The stations were the single-storey wooden structures so typical of the SER.

The line pursued a placid existence with purely local functions, the epitome of the rural branch line that has now passed away. In 1924 there were six weekday trains each way with a short working from the Folkestone direction to Elham and back. By 1937 there were only five through northbound trains and three short workings which went only as far as Lyminge. There was, however, a Sunday service of six trains each way. The 18.54 on weekdays from Shorncliffe was mixed. Although not advertised as such, some trains ran in a circle from Dover back to Dover via Elham, Canterbury, Minster and Deal.

World War II was the most eventful period in the line's history. The northern section was used by a rail-mounted heavy gun, 'Boche Buster'. In 1940 the line was closed to all traffic between Lyminge and Harbledown and was taken over by the Army. Goods trains were operated primarily for military purposes, serving the camps and depots along the line. But public traffic was also carried to and from the various stations. The Army also ran trains for leave purposes, on which ordinary fare paying passengers were allowed. The passenger service to Lyminge was withdrawn in 1943. Passenger services reinstated in 1946 were poorly patronised and were withdrawn from 16 June 1947.

The Feud in the Medway Towns

TOOMER LOOP AND CHATHAM CENTRAL

When the trains from Charing Cross to Gillingham and beyond stop at Strood on the west bank of the Medway, ahead of them can be seen the overbridge carrying the ex-LCDR line across the SER to Maidstone West. On starting, the Gillingham trains diverge from the Maidstone line and climb a steeply-graded and sharply-curved spur round to join the Chatham line. This spur is often called the 'Toomer Loop', immortalising a former Mayor of Rochester, whose name is rather unexpectedly preserved as a result of the Feud. The present spur has replaced the original Toomer Loop on a different alignment.

The East Kent Railway Act of 1853 conferred the right to use the SER station at Strood. Its heaviest engineering work was the Medway Bridge, just downstream of the road bridge, which was then being rebuilt. At the western end of the

Medway bridge the line traversed a 12 chain curve down a 1 in 52 gradient to join the SER, the constraints being the bridge at one end and Strood station at the other. The East Kent was opened between Faversham and Chatham on 25 January 1858, but part of the embankment on the curve to Strood collapsed and delayed opening until 29 March, a horse-bus meanwhile linking Strood and Chatham stations.

Later in 1858 the East Kent obtained powers to link up with the Mid-Kent (Bromley and St Mary Cray). The SER brought that on itself, as it opposed an application for running powers to Dartford, where there would have been a new line to connect with the West End of London & Crystal Palace Railway. The extension involved a sharp curve between the end of the Medway Bridge, where the line turned south to climb the side of the valley to Sole Street at 1 in 100. This was always an awkward spot for LCDR trains.

With the opening of this line in 1860 the sparse service down to Strood dwindled to a daily freight train. The LCDR provided a station just west of the junction with the Strood spur and called it Rochester Bridge. The SER continued its horse-bus from Strood to Chatham. The inconvenience of all this spurred Alderman Toomer, then Mayor of Rochester, to lay a complaint before the Railway Commission in 1876. He made his point, but it required four Orders from the Commission before a through service was started in April 1877. Henceforward the spur was the 'Toomer Loop'.

One of the many proposals for union between the warring companies petered out in 1878. Plans were mounted by the SER for independent access to Chatham. Authorisation was obtained in 1881, but financial difficulties prevented a start on the mile-long branch, as costly as it was short. The powers were revived in 1888 and the line was opened to Rochester Common on 20 July 1891 and to Chatham Central on 1 March 1892. The junction was at the very platform ends at Strood and the line paralleled the Toomer Loop up to a new Medway Bridge immediately below that of the Chatham. Beyond the bridge the line was on a wooden and brick viaduct.

The only intermediate station, located on Gas House Road, was known originally as Rochester, then as Rochester Central and finally as Rochester Common. Beyond, the viaduct crossed the ramp down to Chatham goods depot (ex-LCDR). Chatham Central (actually in the centre of Rochester) was in Rochester High Street just east of the LCDR bridges.

In the year that the branch went into service, the LCDR opened its Rochester station on the site of the present one. The Chatham Central line was an obvious white elephant and the Fusion allowed closure on 1 October 1911. Meanwhile, a connection between the branch and the LCDR had been

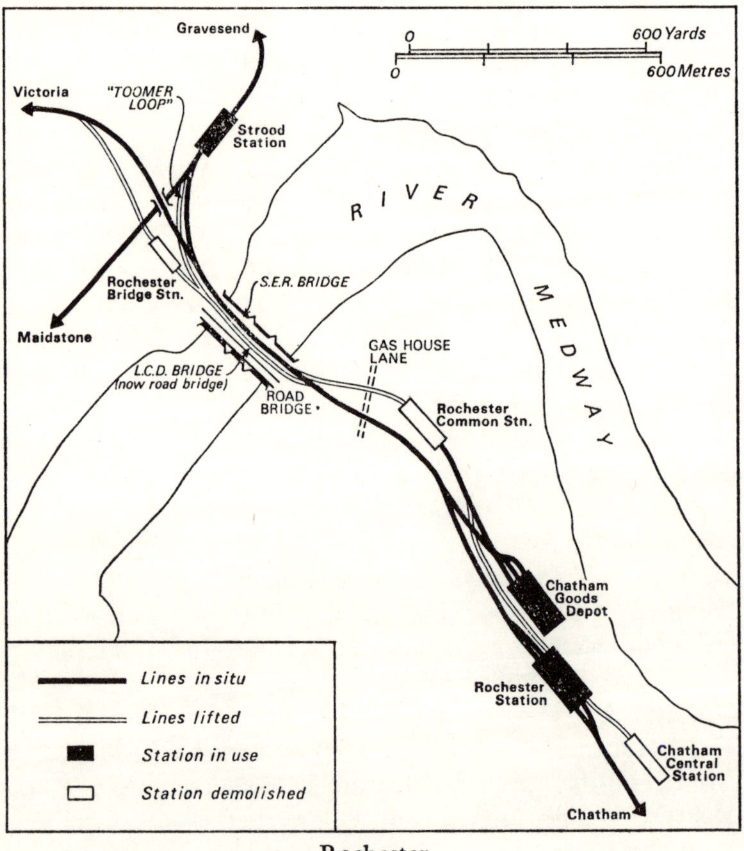

Rochester

laid at the eastern end of the bridge. SER trains for Chatham and beyond were then diverted from the original Toomer Loop, which was put out of use. This is the present route, so its popular name of Toomer Loop is not strictly accurate.

To complete briefly the tangled history of this area—Rochester Bridge Station was rebuilt in 1908, but closed in 1917, though not demolished until 1968 to make way for the approach to the new road bridge. After the Chatham Central closure, Rochester was rebuilt with four tracks and two island platforms, the widening impinging on the right of way of the Chatham Central line. A fire in 1919 damaged the SER bridge so the original Toomer Loop came back into temporary use in 1922 until repairs could be completed. In 1927 the Southern eased the curve on the LCDR main line by diverting the latter across a new bridge over the Maidstone line and on to the SER bridge, thus obliterating the original Toomer Loop. In 1942 the derelict LCDR bridge was strengthened, so it could be used if the SER bridge was damaged by bombing. Finally, the LCDR bridge was demolished to make way for the new road bridge (using the original foundations) which was opened in 1970.

CHAPTER 8

In Search of Deep Water

Our area, bounded as it is by the shores of the Channel, Straits of Dover and Thames Estuary, has had vital port functions throughout history. We have only to think of the Roman ports of Reculver, Richborough and Pevensey, the Mediaeval Cinque Ports, and the modern ferry terminals of Dover, Folkestone and Newhaven, or the oil terminal at Grain. There are also glimpses into the future: the Lighter Aboard Ship (LASH) terminal at Sheerness and the Hovercraft terminal (now used only for maintenance) at Pegwell Bay, hard by where St Augustine landed at Ebbsfleet.

It is scarcely surprising that the objective of much nineteenth-century railway promotion was connected with this port activity, lines being built either to serve existing ports or to develop new ones. Dover was the prime objective of the SER and the first branch (opened in fact before the main line) of the Brighton line was to the port of Shoreham. But not all the railways were as successful as these. Many languished as minor branch lines, never fulfilling their destined purpose. One or two saw a revival from unforeseen causes. The Hundred of Hoo branch (p 129) remains in use by block trains of aggregates and oil. But many more finally succumbed to join the list of forgotten railways, either because they have been robbed of what little port traffic they had, or because the port schemes never reached fruition.

At this point a word of caution is needed. The classification by theme, employed in this book, has many uses. But it must always be remembered that lines had multiple purposes, and also that purposes changed over the years. Thus the story of the line to Dungeness (p 97) could properly be told here, for it originated as a combined railway and port scheme. The latter function was stillborn and the line survived to serve the small seaside resorts on the New Romney section. Again, the story of the Gravesend Railway told below could properly belong to the previous chapter on the Feud. However, the theme of this chapter does provide a link to join mention of widely scattered short lengths of line.

Tapping the Lighter Traffic on the Thames

Traditionally the Port of London relied heavily on lighter transport. Ships, whether berthed at riverside quays or in the enclosed dock systems, discharged much of their cargo into lighters for onward transit to other and often distant quays. It was not until after 1960 that, in the face of lorry competition, lighter traffic fell away so drastically. In 1963 13 million tons of cargo were handled by lighter, but by 1972 only 3·8 million.

It was not necessary for railway companies to be physically linked with shipping berths. The Surrey Docks, for instance, could do perfectly well without rail connection. All that was needed was for a line to be laid to a lighter quay. The LSWR and LCDR were fortunate in that their chief goods depots, Nine Elms and Blackfriars respectively, were located on the river and could be provided with lighter quays.

The LBSCR had two riverside outlets, one at Battersea Wharf, where it also had a goods depot on the approach lines to Victoria, and the other at Deptford Wharf. The powers for a line $\frac{7}{8}$ mile long to the latter were obtained as early as 1846 and it went into service on 2 July 1849. This underlines the importance placed by railway companies on a riverside outlet. The branch left the up side of the main line north of New Cross Gate, descending the side of the embankment to the Grand Surrey Canal which it crossed by a swing bridge. Passing under the South Eastern line from New Cross, from which the formation can still clearly be seen, it ran to a dock with a 500ft frontage and a riverside frontage of 400ft. When the South London Line was opened in 1866 a spur was provided from the original Deptford Wharf line to join it just north of the former Old Kent Road station.

An interesting spur connected the Deptford Wharf branch with the Royal Victoria Victualling Yard. It was laid along Grove Street and was worked by Southern Railway locomotives. Small ex-LBSCR tank engines hauling a few wagons would wander down the street between the houses, while milk-floats dodged round them.

The LBSCR built up a considerable coal trade. Coal brought coastwise from Tyne and Tees, transferred to rail at Deptford Wharf, would be distributed as far as Brighton. In later years the main traffic was of block coal trains to power-stations and gas-works on the line between West Croydon and Mitcham Junction. The branch was closed on 1 January 1964.

Mention must also be made of the SER branch from the North Kent line just south of Charlton Junction, to Angerstein Wharf. This was opened in 1852 by the industrialist who gave his name to the wharf, and it was bought by the SER in 1898. It is still in use for the shipping of scrap-iron and the loading of aggregate brought in by boat.

Further downstream, just east of Erith, a branch led down to a riverside wharf from North End sidings. This again was used to distribute by rail coal which had been brought in coastwise. The coal was forwarded to local goods depots in the south eastern suburbs and particularly by block trains to Lower Sydenham gas-works on the Addiscombe line.

To Gravesend

The important riverside town of Gravesend was reached by the North Kent line of the SER in 1849. The London Tilbury & Southend also reached it in 1854 by means of a ferry from Tilbury Riverside. This was always worked as an extension of their service from Fenchurch Street, and was competitive in both price and time.

25. All that remained in 1974 of the Stationmaster's House at Chatham Central. The view looks over the site of the station towards the present Rochester Station.
26. Petroleum trains still rumble through the site of Sharnal Street Station, where the shell of the Stationmaster's house was all that remained. The formation of the Chatterden Naval Tramway bears away to the left.

Forgotten South Eastern Railway termini in Thanet
27. Ramsgate Town while still a station. *(Tonbridge Historical Society)*
28. The former Margate Sands Station in new guise as a café/casino in 1958.

There was no commercial justification for a third route, but by an Act of 18 July 1881 the nominally-independent Gravesend Railway was incorporated to build a $4\frac{7}{8}$ mile branch from Fawkham Junction, $2\frac{1}{8}$ miles west of Farningham Road, on the LCDR main line. Another Act of 24 July 1882 authorised a pier at Gravesend served by a seven-chain extension. The LCDR took over the Gravesend Company the following year. The ceremonial opening was on 17 April 1886, but public traffic did not begin until 10 May.

As so often the case, the LCDR arrived too late on the scene. For the Gravesend–London traffic the branch was unable to compete with the LTSR or even with the SER. The line adjoined the famous Rosherville Pleasure Gardens and a station was provided. The gardens had been opened in 1840 and served by steamer. Although on Whit Monday 1886 14,000 people visited the gardens, many by the new branch, patronage was already declining. The gardens were finally closed in 1890. Until 1939 West Street Pier was used by the Batavier Line to pick up and set down passengers on its daily London–Rotterdam service, but the traffic was light. The author well recalls the evening boat train passing Bickley, invariably made up of a non-corridor 'Birdcage-trio C' set and a 'loose' corridor coach, the whole in the charge of a C class 0–6–0.

Initially there were fourteen down weekday trains, but the frequency was drastically reduced by the SECR. In 1909 there were only six on Mondays to Fridays, seven on Saturdays and two on Sundays. All these, except one Sunday train, were through from London. In 1913 pull-and-push trains were introduced, and in Southern days few services other than the boat trains were through ones. In 1925, of the twelve down weekday trains, three were from Holborn Viaduct, two from Victoria, one from Bickley, five from Swanley Junction and one from Charing Cross via the Chislehurst Loop. The boat train left Victoria at 17.45 calling only at Penge East, Beckenham Junction, Shortlands and Bromley South, running non-stop thence to Gravesend.

After electrification of the main line in 1939, the branch trains were cut back to Swanley or Farningham Road. In 1952 there were only five weekday departures, four from Swanley and one from Farningham Road. On Saturdays however there were ten services, three from Swanley and seven from Farningham Road. Passenger trains were withdrawn on 3 August 1953.

Fawkham Junction was marked only by a signal box. The double track curved away to the north. Three-quarters of a mile beyond was Longfield Halt, opened in 1913 and located in a chalk cutting. Fawkham station was remote from that village, but slap in the middle of Longfield, the Halt being distinctly peripheral. It was only logical that in 1961 Fawkham became 'Longfield for Fawkham and Hartley'. The branch line ran almost dead straight through orchards and market gardens to Southfleet, 2½ miles from Fawkham. This was an island platform with all the buildings, including the booking office, on the platform.

The line crossed the A2 by a modern girder bridge, and soon afterwards crossed the North Kent Line. Rosherville station, though closed on 15 July 1933, survived intact in 1953. In that year coal sidings and a connection to Bowaters Paper Mill were in use. Gravesend (Gravesend West Street from 1900 and Gravesend West from 1950) was half a mile further on. It had a V-shaped layout, the northerly platform curving away to the pier, on which there was a separate platform. The goods depot was on the south side and the Southern concentrated all traffic on this, closing the ex-SER depot at Gravesend Central.

After closure to passengers the line was singled. Gravesend West was closed to freight on 24 March 1968 and the line was cut back to Southfleet, where a large coal railhead was established. Block trains with coal for cement plants (each of which was rail-connected) were run from the Midlands, final delivery being by road. It was the height of the BRB 'hatred' of private sidings. After the opening of the large centralised APCM plant at Northfleet in 1970, adapted for the 'merry-go-round' system, the depot closed. But in 1985 the overgrown track and the bridge across the A2 remained.

Port Victoria and Queenborough

The LCDR line to Sheerness was opened in 1860. In 1875 the company persuaded the Zealand Steamship Company to transfer the Ramsgate terminal of its Flushing service to Sheerness Pier. On 15 May 1876 a permanent terminal was opened, at Queenborough Pier, reached by a short branch from the Sheerness line diverging just north of Queenborough station. The advantage to the LCDR was that Queenborough was outside the area covered by the 1865 Agreement, though it was a breach of the spirit if not of the letter.

The SER therefore supported the Hundred of Hoo Company (p 122), formed to build a line from the North Kent to deep water opposite Queenborough. This was a period of *rapprochement* between the SER and the LCDR, the former advising the small company to seek powers to build only as far as Stoke, which were obtained in 1879. By then the big companies had again fallen out, and an Act for the extension to the Medway was obtained the following year. In 1881 the Hundred of Hoo was taken over by the SER.

The terminal pier was nowhere near any habitation. To vie with the Chatham's terminal at Queenborough (named after Philippa, wife of Edward III), the SER hit on the title of Port Victoria. Watkin described the pier as the beginning of a great port. Seventy years later his prophecy was fulfilled, but not in the way he expected. The eleven miles of single track from Hoo Junction were opened to Sharnal Street on 1 April 1882 and throughout on 11 September. Ferry connections were provided to Queenborough and to Sheerness. But although the route was only forty-two miles from London against the fifty-two by LCDR metals, little traffic was obtained.

Queenborough Pier was burned down in 1900, and for some months the Flushing steamers were diverted to Port Victoria. In 1901 the ferry service was withdrawn. Trains

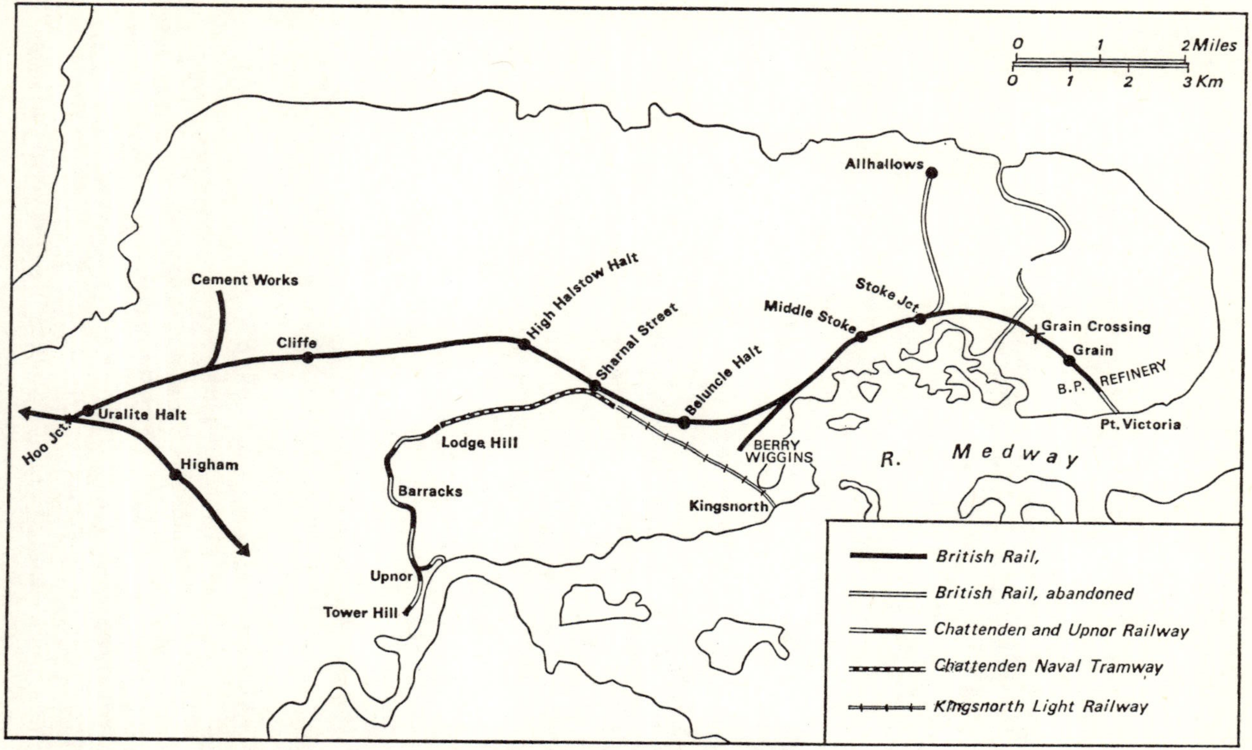

The Hundred of Hoo (1970)

continued to run as the Royal Corinthian Yacht Club was nearby, and there was no road access to it. In 1916 the pier was considered unsafe and the seaward end was barricaded off. 1931 saw it closed altogether, a short platform being provided at the landward end. After World War II the site was swallowed up by the Grain Oil Refinery. A new station was provided at Grain (opened 4 September 1951), just east of Grain Crossing Halt, and the twice-daily train service terminated there until passenger services ceased on 3 December 1961.

Queenborough Pier was closed in 1914. After World War I when the Flushing steamers were reinstated, their British terminal was transferred to Parkeston Quay. A brief reopening in 1923 when Kingsferry Bridge was damaged was the final one. The pier was later dismantled, though the foundations can be seen at low tide. Until the refinery closed in 1982 supertankers unloaded at the site of Port Victoria, bringing the Port of Medway into the front rank of British ports. Refined products are still landed and railed, as are sea-dredged aggregates at Cliffe. Watkin was not completely mistaken in his vision.

Some minor branches

FAVERSHAM QUAY

The Act of 1853, incorporating the East Kent Railway, authorised a 1¼ mile branch to Faversham Quay. Faversham has a long history as a port. It was a limb of the Cinque Ports and even today has quite a considerable trade. The branch was opened for freight traffic on 12 April 1860. When the small wayside station at Faversham assumed its present form in the 1880s, a new goods depot was provided with access off the branch. Further down there was a sleeper depot and the line ended on a wharf at the far end of Abbey Street. A visit in 1964 showed the line still in situ and in use as far as the sleeper depot, but it has since been taken up from about 200yd north of the bridge over the Whitstable road.

HAMPTON PIER (HERNE BAY)

Few visitors to Hampton Pier on the western outskirts of Herne Bay realise that it was the terminus of a long siding from the LCDR line three-quarters of a mile to the south. It was constructed by the Herne Bay, Hampton & Reculver Oyster Fishery Company, which received powers to build the pier in 1864. The line was used for the companies' own traffic using horse and sail traction. The pier and line were sold in 1881.

RICHBOROUGH

Mention has already been made of Richborough (p 39), at the mouth of the Stour. This was developed during World War I for military traffic to supplement Dover and Folkestone. A train-ferry was inaugurated in 1917, the vessels being used after the war to start the Harwich–Zeebrugge service. The port was reached from the SECR by a siding off the Minster–Deal line, facing the Minster direction. This is in use as far as the main road for access to the new Richborough power station. The gates where the lines crossed the A256 to the quays were still there in 1974, but were later swept away in road-widening. The right-of-way could be traced along the river bank to the quay by Pfizer's factory. Ammunition specials were run from Faversham (where there was a large munitions plant at Oare) via a spur connecting the LCDR and the SER lines west of Canterbury and thence via Minster. This spur was reinstated during World War II and again after the Kent Coast floods of 1953. Richborough port was also approached from the south along a line later connected with the East Kent Light Railway (p 39).

Canterbury and Whitstable

Although in some senses it was not the orthodox 'classical' railway which the Liverpool & Manchester was, the Canterbury & Whitstable was opened in the same year as the L&M, 1830. It was only six miles long, but its place in the railway history of Southern England is assured, for it was the first public, steam-powered, passenger and freight line in the South of England. It is discussed here because it was built as Canterbury's outlet to the sea.

In 1820 Canterbury was the most important town in East Kent, and the largest market. Much of its longer-distance trade was by water and for this the city depended on its river, the Stour, and its small port at the head of navigation, Fordwich. Silting was an old problem, and from the reign of Henry VIII onwards there were periodic proposals for a river navigation. The last of these was a plan prepared by Telford, for which an Act was obtained in 1825.

However, that doughty prophet of the Railway Age, William James, had visited Canterbury in 1823 and urged on the city council the desirability of a railway outlet direct to the Thames estuary. His arguments were so persuasive that he was asked to prepare a survey. A Bill was promoted in competition with the one for the Stour Navigation, and on 10 June 1825 the Act incorporating the Canterbury & Whitstable Railway Company received the Royal Assent. Doubts on the adequacy of the estimates prepared by James led to George Stephenson being called in. He confirmed the alignment suggested by James, but increased the estimated cost by £6,000 to £32,000. Offered the post of engineer, he delegated the task of laying-out the line to Joseph Locke (later engineer to the Grand Junction and the London & Southampton Railways), and that of building it to John Dixon. Work was suspended in 1827 through lack of funds and when it was restarted Robert Stephenson took charge. The ceremonial opening was on 3 May 1830. Public traffic began next day. The company made several attempts to lease the line to another operator, finally succeeding when the SER began to work it from 29 September 1844, absorbing the C&W company by the Act of 4 August 1853.

The line was single and was just over six miles long. It was very steeply graded and was worked by stationary engines. The famous *Invicta* locomotive built by Robert Stephenson was used only over the last 1¾ miles at the Whitstable end. In 1839 it was withdrawn and the whole line was cable-worked until locomotives took over on 6 April 1846.

The original terminus was in North Lane, just outside the city walls and to the north of Westgate Towers. When the SER line was opened in 1846, to avoid a level crossing, the C&W was diverted to a short bay at the country end of the down platform of Canterbury West station. North Lane station disappeared under the goods yard, which was laid out between the main line and North Lane. The entrance to the coal depot from North Lane is almost certainly the site of the original station.

Canterbury lies in the valley of the Stour, where the river is about 25ft above sea level. To the north, athwart any route to the coast at Whitstable, is the London Clay plateau of the Blean which rises to over 200ft. The heavy soils are not very fertile and the Blean is still heavily forested. Immediately upon leaving Canterbury West the track of the C&W climbed steeply through the suburbs of Canterbury, first at 1 in 76, then increasing to 1 in 41 and 1 in 47.

After ¾ mile was the southern portal of the 828yd Tyler Hill Tunnel. Many 'popular' railway histories quote a long-standing myth that the tunnel was demanded by the promoters as a feature of any 'good' railway. There is no written evidence, and a short investigation in the field reveals there was no practical alternative to the tunnel. This, however, had a very limited bore, and nothing wider than 9ft 3in or higher than 11ft 0in could pass, which placed severe limits on what locomotives or rolling stock could be used. Tayleur 0–6–0s of the 119 class were used after 1846. In 1883 two Stirling O class 0–6–0s were given cut-down chimneys. After 1890 four R class 0–6–0Ts were given cut-down boiler mountings and these worked the line until closure in 1952. Very elderly four-wheeled coaches were used. In 1919 there was a set of four ex-LCDR four wheelers, but in the 1920s bogie coaches were used. Only open goods wagons were possible. The tunnel made its presence felt as late as 1974, when a collapse twenty-two years after closure damaged university buildings erected over it.

The gradient through the tunnel was 1 in 56. On emerging into the open it steepened to 1 in 49. At $1\frac{3}{4}$ miles from Canterbury West the line crossed on the level the by-road from Tyler Hill to Blean. Just to the north was the summit of the line and here the first of the stationary engines, Tyler Hill engine, was located. Just beyond the level crossing was Blean & Tyler Hill Halt, opened in January 1908.

The line descended very gently at 1 in 848 for three-quarters of a mile to the site of Clowes Wood engine, where there was a passing place. The gradient steepened to 1 in 63 and after a short distance to 1 in 31 and 1 in 28 to a point north of Bogshole, where between 1830 and 1839 the locomotive was attached to trains. For a short while there was a stationary engine at Bogshole, but later the incline was amalgamated with Clowes Wood.

There was a level stretch of half a mile to South Street. The gradients beyond proved too steep for *Invicta* and a stationary engine was installed. At the level crossing was South Street Halt, opened in October 1911; its site is commemorated by a shop, 'The Halt Stores'.

The line dropped at 1 in 57 and 1 in 50 down to the outskirts of Whitstable, passing under the Thanet Way (A299) by means of an imposing concrete bridge with space for double track, and provided when the road was built in 1935. The line crossed Church Street over a bridge with a very narrow arch which was demolished fairly recently. Beyond, it crossed the LCDR. On 1 January 1915 the present Whitstable & Tankerton station was opened half a mile east of the 1860 LCDR station. In July 1914 a halt was opened on the C&W just north of the overbridge, connected by steps down the embankment to the main line station.

The line swung round to cross the main road on the level. On the landward side was the single-platform station opened in February 1894 which even in the 1950s retained its wooden building as a Sea Scout headquarters. There was a short run-round loop. Immediately across the road was the station provided by the SER in 1846, and a large fan of sidings serving the south and east sides of the harbour. The original 1830 terminus was adjacent to the 'Steam Packet Inn'.

The harbour was built in connection with the railway, a small basin excavated out of the mud in the foreshore. It was used for the import of coal, timber and grain. In later years the latter, conveyed in converted open wagons to a mill in Canterbury, formed the principal traffic on the daily freight train.

Passenger services were infrequent and slow, while the coaches were old and uncomfortable. In 1925 there were nine weekday round trips (ten on Saturdays) and seven on summer Sundays. It suffered greatly from bus competition after World War I and the service was withdrawn from 1 January 1931. The freight service was withdrawn from 1 December 1952, but was temporarily re-instated the following year to bring coal to Whitstable while the main line was cut by the March floods.

In 1958 Whitstable Harbour was sold by the British Transport Commission for £12,000 to the Whitstable and Tankerton Urban District Council. There was indignation among ratepayers and a widespread feeling the Council had taken on a bad bargain, but the yachting boom was under way and has continued ever since. In addition the small ports of South East England were experiencing a revival in the cargo trade, and regular services were established to Denmark and Holland. By 1970 Whitstable Harbour was busier than it had ever been. It was the BTC which had had the worst of the bargain.

Other port branches

DOVER HARBOUR

Dover Harbour had two interesting lines which deserve mention. The connection with the dockside lines trailed into the LCDR line in the short gap between the harbour tunnel and the harbour station. When the Prince of Wales Pier was built in 1900–1902 the dock lines were extended across a new bridge over the entrance to Wellington Dock and along the pier to a small station at the end. The Hamburg–Amerika liner *Deutschland* called between 1902 and 1909 and connecting boat trains were run.

In 1907 a coal and petroleum depot was opened on the new eastern arm. This was provided with a railway line trailing in to the Prince of Wales Pier and traversing the length of the promenade, Waterloo Crescent. Eventually a direct connection was laid in. In later years factories were built at the Eastern Docks and some general freight as well as coal and oil was worked along Dover's sea front, the P class 0–6–0T and more recently the diesel shunter being preceded by a man with a red flag, whose duties included rounding-up drivers of cars parked across the line. In the 1950s accompanied car traffic began to increase and the constant additions to the ferry terminal at the Eastern Docks cut back other activities, and rail traffic ceased in 1966.

The eastern arm is part of the great harbour of refuge built between 1897–1909. To bring in materials, the contractors built a line from Martin Mill on the Dover–Deal line. The single track ran over the surface of the high chalk plateau parallel with the main line which climbs up to the summit just at the entrance to Guston tunnel. From there it bore away to the top of the cliffs 350ft above the sea. It then descended in a zig-zag on a vertigious shelf cut into the sheer cliff. At the end of its useful life it was hoped to convert it to a passenger-carrying line and the Dover and Martin Mill Light Railway Order was obtained. In World War II much of the formation was used by a military line connecting Martin Mill with cliff-top batteries.

RYE HARBOUR

When the Ashford–Hastings line was opened on 13 February 1851 a branch was provided to Rye Harbour. Opened in 1854, a single line trailed into the southbound line $\frac{3}{8}$ mile south of Rye station. It was used only for freight and was worked as a siding. Just under two miles long, it crossed the Rye–

Hastings road (A259) on the level and ran across the marshes parallel with the road to Rye Harbour, crossing it on the level just outside the village. It ended at a short pier on the River Rother opposite the Rye & Camber station (p 146). It was used to carry flints brought from Dungeness by boat and to serve an oil firm and a chemical works with private sidings. By 1955 it was almost derelict, and it has since been completely taken up, though the route can easily be traced.

NEWHAVEN

At Newhaven, the western shore of the Ouse estuary was served by the tramway built in connection with the harbour improvements of 1878. It diverged at the level crossing over the A259 coast road and shared the swing-bridge over the river. A1 Terrier 0–6–0Ts were the only locomotives allowed over it. The survival of the line, which was closed in 1963, and two other lines, the Kent & East Sussex, and the Hayling Island branch, certainly prolonged the active life of these locomotives.

SHOREHAM (KINGSTON WHARF)

The only rail outlet to the busy Shoreham Harbour was at Kingston Wharf. Kingston-on-Sea station was opened with the Shoreham branch from Brighton in 1840 and was closed in 1879. Five and a quarter miles from Brighton, it was situated halfway between Southwick and Shoreham stations. There was a short rope-worked incline to the wharf with turntable access at each end. Shunting on the wharf was by horse. In 1938 a locomotive worked incline was provided and used until 1968.

LITTLEHAMPTON

When opening its branch to Littlehampton in 1863 the LBSCR had ideas of developing trade from Littlehampton Harbour. By 1861 there were regular sailings to the Channel Islands and Harfleur. Sidings were therefore provided to the harbour, but shipping services declined and the port was closed in 1939, having since reopened for aggregate traffic.

CHAPTER 9

A Miscellany of Lost Causes

There remain a few forgotten lines which have not been mentioned because they do not fit into the various categories dealt with so far. There is therefore no real connecting link, other than the melancholy fact they outlived their original functions and found no new ones in replacement.

The Westerham Valley

The small market town of Westerham lies at the foot of the North Downs where the east–west Sevenoaks–Reigate road (A25) crosses the road from Bromley to Edenbridge (A233, B2026). Before the area became popular for commuters, which led to a considerable growth of the town and surrounding villages, it was unimportant and isolated. Five miles to the south was Edenbridge station (1842) on the old SER main line, and as far away to the east was Sevenoaks, opened in 1868. Westerham in the middle nineteenth century was like many similar towns up and down the country. Left aside by railway development, it sought a branch line to connect it with the main line. The Westerham branch was typical of many similar branches in its history, but because of the geography and the close network of through lines in South East England it is not typical of this area.

As was so often the case, it was local enterprise that promoted the Westerham Valley Railway, incorporated by the Act of 24 July 1876. The subscribers were concerned with the general economic development of the area rather than with the expectation of the line itself being profitable. The line was single and ran for nearly five miles from Dunton Green, on the main line through Sevenoaks, to a terminus on the A233 on the very edge of Westerham. It was opened on 7 July 1881, the company having been absorbed by the SER in that year.

At Dunton Green the branch trailed into the up line. There was a separate platform on the branch and a run-round loop. Leaving the station the line bore away westward under the A21 and ran along the fertile Vale of Holmesdale, with the scarp of the Downs to the north and the wooded Ragstone hills to the south. One and a quarter miles from Dunton Green was the short concrete platform of the unstaffed Chevening Halt, the site now completely obliterated by the new bridge by which the lane crosses the A21(M). The only intermediate station was at Brasted, three miles from Dunton Green. It had a single platform and small goods yard, but no passing loop. Westerham had a single platform with a single-storey timber building typical of the SER. There was a loop and a goods yard.

Trains were controlled by electric tablet, so that two could be in service at peak periods. The line had only local functions, but the service was always a good one. In 1925 there were sixteen weekday departures from Westerham, with an extra trip on Mondays, Wednesdays and Thursdays, and ten on Sundays. Soon after that, Westerham shed was closed, the locomotives being shedded at Tonbridge. The pull-and-push trains provided a self-contained service, though when shifts were changed the whole train was taken down to Tonbridge, providing a local service on the main line.

By 1952 there were twenty-two departures from Dunton Green on weekdays, twenty on Saturdays and fifteen on Sundays. By then although off-peak traffic was very light, there were 80 to 100 commuters, but with the elimination of steam, providing rolling stock for the Westerham line would be difficult. Closure notices were posted but considerable opposition, principally from the commuters, was aroused. At the subsequent inquiry the Transport Users' Consultative

Committee recommended against closure, but the Minister of Transport, the Rt Hon Ernest (later Lord) Marples, overruled them. The Marples–Beeching era was setting in. Closure took place on 30 October 1961. Attempts were made to float a preservation society, but the Sevenoaks By-Pass (A21(M)) was being planned. On the excuse of a slight saving from not providing a bridge, the right-of-way of the Westerham Valley railway could be irrevocably severed, and then conveniently forgotten. Indeed most of its course has now disappeared under the M25.

To the Devil's Dyke

The Devil's Dyke is a deep and spectacular combe in the scarp of the South Downs, and it has always been a popular spot for holidaymakers staying at Brighton. The 3½ mile branch was promoted solely to develop this tourist traffic, as there would be no local sources of traffic. On 2 August 1877 the Brighton & Dyke Railway Company was incorporated. Sufficient capital was slow in forthcoming and opening was delayed until 1 September 1887, too late for the summer peak.

The site of Dyke Junction is two miles west of Brighton, immediately west of Aldrington Halt, which was called Dyke Junction from its opening in 1905 until 1932. The alignment of the branch is indicated by the layout of Harrington's premises. After passing under the A27, and half a mile from Dyke Junction, was Rowan Halt, opened on 18 December 1933 to serve a housing estate.

The line climbed steeply up the slopes of the South Downs mainly at 1in 40/41, for there was a rise of some 400ft in the 3½ miles. There were few earthworks, curves being frequent and sharp. As the train blasted up the bare hills it gave the impression of climbing a mountain line. It ran through a typical area of the South Downs, open rolling treeless country with immense fields and only an occasional farmstead with huge barns.

A mile short of the terminus a private halt was provided to serve the nearby golf course. The Dyke station had a single platform with a corrugated-iron station and a run-round loop. A path climbed steeply up to the road, the toiling passenger being rewarded by the sight of the bus speeding on its way from Brighton to the Dyke Hotel nearly a mile away, and 300ft higher than the station.

The line was therefore very vulnerable to bus competition. In 1925 there were six weekday trips and four on Sundays, all of which ran to and from Brighton. After 1933 a number of extra trips were provided to Rowan Halt. These latter had to be pull-and-push trains as there was no run-round loop. The Dyke trains were not operated on the pull-and-push system and in the 1930s consisted of a single open 'Balloon' trailer. From 1933 to 1934 the line was worked by the one Sentinel–Cammell railcar that the Southern ever owned. In 1934 it was tranferred to the Westerham branch for a short time. The line was closed between 1 January 1917 until 26 July 1920. It could make no contribution to the war effort. Although it had always been worked by the LBSCR the line remained independent until it was unwillingly absorbed by the Southern in 1923. It was closed from 1 January 1939.

Kemp Town

In our area only Brighton was large enough to support self-contained suburban services, although of course short-distance inter-urban services, such as that between Brighton and Worthing, were and still are an important aspect of operations. One suburban service within the Brighton and Hove conurbation was to Rowan Halt (above). The other and more important was one of $2\frac{3}{8}$ miles from Brighton to Kemp Town. The latter station served a large building estate developed between 1823 and 1850 and called after a former Lord of the Manor.

On 13 May 1864 the LBSCR received authority to build a branch from Kemp Town Junction, on the Brighton–Lewes

29. A transfer trip from the Eastern arm of Dover Harbour was held up while the Pilotman requests a van driver to clear the line. 1960.
30. Nowadays the bulldozer is liable to obliterate old rail lines, but the embankment of the Sandgate branch, closed in 1931, was left intact, and bungalows were perched on it.

31. A special train, run by the Stephenson Locomotive Society on 23 June 1956 leaves the tunnel and enters Kemp Town Station, then a freight depot. *(R. C. Riley)*

32. Dunton Green station from the north in 1891. The Westerham bay is on the right. *(Tonbridge Historical Society)*

line, for $1\frac{3}{8}$ miles southward to the northern edge of Kemp Town. It was opened on 2 August 1869 with a service of nine round trips. By 1883 there were seventeen trips, a typical train being of five close-coupled four-wheelers hauled by a 'Terrier'. On 1 January 1906 a more intensive service of thirty-two trips on an interval basis was inaugurated, operated by 48 seater petrol railcars. These were soon replaced by pull-and-push trains of a single third class 'Balloon' trailer-coach and a D1 0–4–2T.

The service was suspended on 1 January 1917 and not restored until 10 August 1919. This suspension, coupled with the introduction of bus services direct to the town centre, proved disastrous. In spite of a frequency increased to thirty-six weekday trips, closure became inevitable and took place after the last train on 31 December 1932. The event was overshadowed by a more important one: it was the last day of the steam service from London. Freight services continued, the whole line becoming a siding on 29 July 1933, until they were finally withdrawn on 14 June 1971 and most of the line dismantled.

Brighton is built on a very hilly site. Two deep and steep-sided valleys, one allowing access to the town by the London Road, the other by the Lewes Road, converge on the Old Steine gardens. The town has extended inland up the valleys and over the adjacent Downs. Brighton station is built on the west side of the combined valley. The Lewes line crosses the London Road valley by a spectacular viaduct and there is only the length of London Road Station (opened 10 January 1877) between the eastern end and Ditchling Road tunnel which takes the line through to the Lewes Road valley.

The branch, though very short, had equally heavy engineering features. Kemp Town Junction was immediately beyond the tunnel. The branch curved away southward over the fourteen-arch Lewes Road viaduct, a counterpart of the London Road one. On the other side was Lewes Road station, opened on 1 September 1873. It had an island platform between the tracks and another platform with the station buildings on the up side, and there was a small goods yard. After closure the station became a pickle factory. From there, the Kemp Town line became single. A quarter of a mile beyond, after crossing a three-arch viaduct over Hartington Road, there was a halt of that name. It was opened for the railcar service, but closed in 1911. Beyond, the line entered the 1,024yd Kemp Town Tunnel to emerge into the terminus.

The passenger station had a single platform with a short bay and a very impressive range of buildings. Clearly, it was expected that other platforms would be built. In the late 1870s a very extensive goods yard was laid out, though it never fulfilled the expectations that it would exceed Brighton in importance as a freight depot. Nevertheless it survived for coal and general goods until 14 June 1971.

The narrow gauge

Narrow-gauge lines, other than purely industrial lines, were most uncommon in South East England. There were, however, two lines which deserve mention here. One was a public line, the other a private line operated by the Admiralty. Almost unknown during its lifetime, the latter is remembered by its rolling stock, which has obtained a new lease of life in far-off Mid-Wales.

THE RYE & CAMBER TRAMWAY

Mention has already been made of the Rye Harbour branch, running from Rye towards the coast on the south side of the Rother. The Rye & Camber Tramway paralleled it on the north bank en route to the little coastal resort of Camber.

In 1894 the Rye Golf Course was established on the dunes opposite Rye Harbour and local businessmen promoted the Rye & Camber Tramways Company, registered on 6 April 1895. The line was built without Parliamentary powers under the supervision of Colonel Stephens and was of 3ft 0in gauge. The 1¾ miles from Rye to Golf Club Halt were opened on 13 July 1895, and proved so successful that after six months a dividend of 7½ per cent on the £2,800 capital was declared. On 13 July 1908 a half-mile extension to Camber Sands was opened.

The station at Rye lay across the river from the town, approached by a path from the A259 just beyond the bridge. The corrugated-iron roofs of the two huts on the platform had 'Tram' and 'Station' painted on them, clearly visible from the town walls crowning the hill on which Rye is built. There was also a run-round loop and two sidings. The line paralleled the road to Camber. Golf Club Halt, a simple structure with a tin shed which still survives, was on the river bank at the ferry from Rye Harbour. Beyond, the line turned inland through the dunes to the even simpler structure of the terminus, which had a run-round loop.

Until a petrol locomotive was introduced in 1925, the line was worked by a W. G. Bagnall 2–4–0T, *Camber*. There were two wooden-bodied coaches. Though suffering from competition from the faster, more comfortable and more convenient buses, services survived until 1939. In 1940 the Forces took over the line and provided a concrete surface along the track between Halfway House and Rye Harbour so that it could be used by road as well as rail vehicles. The Admiralty put the line to some use, but when it was handed back after the war it was unusable and was never restored.

THE CHATTENDEN & UPNOR RAILWAY

We now return to North Kent. Chatham was a military as well as a naval centre. Shortly before the South African War the Royal Engineers laid out the narrow-gauge Chattenden & Upnor railway for training purposes. In 1904 the railway troops were transferred to Longmoor in Hampshire and the Admiralty took over the line.

The 2ft 6in gauge line originated at the waterfront south of Upper Upnor. It climbed steeply past Tank Field, where there was a passing loop and signal box. Another branch led up from a pier at Lower Upnor. The two branches both crossed Lower Upnor Lane on the level to a fully signalled junction just beyond. There was a signal box and a 'station' on the Upper Upnor branch, the latter consisting of metal plates at ground level with a railing at the back. This was used by the Royal Engineers to practise entraining. The site has been obliterated by road improvements.

From Upnor Junction the line climbed steeply at 1 in 30 round the flanks of Beacon Hill to cross the main road to Grain (A228) by an impressive girder bridge. This part of the right of way has been converted into a road. Beyond, the line encircled Chattenden Barracks, where there was a siding, and entered the Lodge Hill ammunition dump.

A description of the line and its locomotives, by J. R. Hayton (*The Railway Magazine*, 1941, volume 87, pp 207–211), describes the Upper Upnor branch as little-used to Tank Field and derelict beyond to its terminus at Tower Hill Camp, but the line was resuscitated during the war, new rolling stock being provided. After the war the line was dieselised. The last scheduled service ran on 19 May 1961 and the line closed altogether on 31 December 1961.

Later in the year, through the good offices of Sir Thomas Salt, rolling stock was made available to the Welshpool & Llanfair Light Railway Preservation Company. Four bogie coaches (built in 1947) and a 'combination car' (with passenger /guard accommodation) of 1957 together with the diesel locomotive *Upnor Castle* of 1954 were transferred to the W&L. *Upnor Castle* was sold to the Festiniog Railway to provide funds to buy *Chattenden*, a 1949 diesel locomotive from the C&U.

The Chattenden Naval Tramway

The C&U entered the Lodge Hill magazines from the south. From the east a standard gauge line emerged, the Chattenden Naval Tramway. This was a single line about two miles long connecting Lodge Hill with the Hundred of Hoo line at Sharnal Street (p 129). In 1901 the Chattenden Naval Tramways Order was signed under the Light Railway Act for a double-track line from Lodge Hill to the water front at Kingsnorth, but only a single line as far as Sharnal Street was built.

In 1915 the line was extended to Kingsnorth pier to serve a munitions factory and airship hangars. After the war, a chemical firm leased part of the munitions factory and the line east of Sharnal Street. On 6 November 1926 the Kingsnorth Light Railway Order was signed to permit the running of a passenger service. By an Order of 25 July 1929 line was transferred to the Kingsnorth Light Railway Company. No public traffic was however handled and with the demise of the chemical firm the line became derelict. Much of it has disappeared under the new power station at Kingsnorth.

The Chattenden Naval Tramway emerged from Lodge Hill to cross the lane from Chattenden to Lodge Hill Farm. It ran down a wide and shallow valley for two miles, when the single track swung round behind Sharnal Street station to cross under the main road (A228). Just beyond was a group of four double-ended exchange sidings with a connection to the main line. At the eastern end the Kingsnorth Light Railway paralleled the main line before the latter diverged to the north east. The KLR ran straight on past Beluncle Farm, through the chemical works to terminate at a pier across the mud flats, the Slede Ooze. At one time there was a connection to Berry Wiggins' Refinery. The latter later had an independent connection with the main line. In 1931 the KLR was worked by an 0–4–0T and a petrol locomotive. There seems to be no record of any CNT motive power.

Stone blocks and iron rails

The Canterbury & Whitstable of 1830 was, as we have seen, scarcely an orthodox railway. Nevertheless it can be taken as the first steam railway in South East England. The area played only a very small part in the development of the pre-steam railway for the two situations favourable for the provision of these lines, mineral workings and canals, which required feeders, were not well represented. Nevertheless, there were two important pre-steam lines in the area, the Surrey Iron Railway and its southerly extension, the Croydon, Merstham & Godstone Railway. These had a combined length of 25¾ miles.

THE SURREY IRON RAILWAY

The Surrey Iron Railway originated in a proposal of 1799 to improve communications between London and Portsmouth by a rail/canal route, the rail section to be open to public transport on payment of toll permitting users to operate their own wagons and horses. In short, it was to be a highly-specialised form of turnpike road.

The northern section of the route, from the Thames at Wandsworth to Croydon, was to be a canal. William Jessop, who was retained as consultant, recommended against this as the water requirements for a canal would be detrimental to the river-based industries, which depended on the power produced from the unimproved river. Sir John Rennie later agreed with Jessop's recommendation. The Wandle Valley was one of London's most important industrial areas. In his 'Survey of Surrey', James Malcolm reported there were thirty-eight industrial plants, employing a total of 1,700 workers and representing an investment upwards of a million pounds. This alone was a sufficient market for an improved transport line, even if the ultimate aim of reaching Portsmouth was never achieved.

On 3 June 1800 the promoters met at Wandsworth and finally decided on a railway rather than a canal. The Act incorporating the Surrey Iron Railway received the Royal Assent on 21 May 1801. It was the world's first public railway, in the sense it was open for the carriage of all freight offering. There were few natural obstacles to construction. William Jessop was appointed engineer, and he and his partner in the Butterley Iron Works, Benjamin Outram, were contractors. The eight miles of line were officially opened on 26 July 1803, though it is probable that public traffic had already been passing to and from 'Mr Henckell's iron mills' at Garrett, about two miles south of Wandsworth.

The Surrey Iron Railway was double track. Recent excavations at Merstham have shown the gauge to be 4ft 6in between the centres of the holes in the stone blocks, which means about 4ft 2in between the insides of the rail flanges. The line was laid with plate rails on stone sleepers, which can still be seen in rockeries and walls. Four-wheeled wagons, with narrow, flangeless iron wheels were used. These were drawn by horses, either singly or coupled into trains. Wagons and horses were provided by merchants and carriers, who paid tolls calculated on commodity, weight and distance. It was basically the same system as that of the turnpike roads, but with a highly specialised track, a railway, and not a road.

The terminus was at wharves and a small dock on the Thames at the mouth of the Wandle. The line followed the course of the Wandle for about 5½ miles to near where Mitcham Junction now is located. Here it bore away from the river and cut across low-lying land to Croydon. A 1¼ mile branch, opened on or about 1 June 1804, followed the river up to Hackbridge.

Beyond Mitcham Junction the right-of-way was for the most part incorporated in the line of the Wimbledon & Croydon Railway, authorised in 1853 and opened in 1855.

On 17 May 1803 the Croydon, Merstham & Godstone Iron Railway Company was incorporated to extend the Surrey Iron Railway up the dry valley extending south of Croydon into the North Downs, through the Merstham Gap in the crest of the Downs and on to Godstone, with a branch to Reigate. The Reigate branch was to be the first stage of the extension through to Portsmouth. In the event, Nelson's victory at Trafalgar removed the French threat to Channel shipping and the urge to reach Portsmouth faded. The line in fact never got beyond Merstham. It was opened in June 1805.

The Croydon, Merstham & Godstone was mostly single

track. Like the Surrey Iron Railway, its course can in large measure still be traced by property boundaries and footpaths. The terminus of the line was in the Greystone Lime Works, a great scar in the face of the North Downs scarp half a mile north of Merstham Station. This was a source of traffic, but the line was never very successful. The LBSCR Act of 1837 compelled the company to purchase the line, which was closed to traffic in 1838, the southern part of the route being destroyed by the deep cuttings on the approach to Merstham Tunnel.

The Surrey Iron Railway lingered until 1846, when an Act of Dissolution was obtained. The preamble stated that 'traffic along the line . . . has of late years been diminishing'. As mentioned, the southern part was incorporated in the Wimbledon & West Croydon line.

Conclusion

The oldest lines in the area have been described last. They have been 'forgotten' for over one and a quarter centuries, yet they have left some traces on the rapidly evolving urban landscape, and the knowledgeable can still pick out sections of their alignments. The same can be said of all the other forgotten railways in the book.

Meanwhile, to finish on one of the themes of the book. A railway line was built in response to a particular demand to fulfil a particular function. Such functions are not static, changing over time in response to social and economic changes in the area that the line serves. If the line is not adapted to these functional changes it becomes redundant, is closed and becomes forgotten. Because so many of the lines in the South East have been adapted to change they have survived. But those which have become 'forgotten' have their own interest and fully deserve some memorial. It is hoped that this book will serve as one.

Gazetteer

The gazetteer has these purposes: (a) to summarise the basic information about each line mentioned in the text, including the opening and closing dates; (b) to list the physical remains of each line; (c) to describe the scenic backgrounds, and to mention the possibilities of visiting the lines.

It must be remembered that the demand for land in South Eastern England is very heavy indeed; the lines are being obliterated at a remarkable rate. The physical remains are listed as they were visited in 1974 (updated by 1985 visits), but changes are so rapid that visitors must be prepared to find that considerable alterations have taken place.

Station houses, offices, goods sheds, etc are being put to other uses and greatly altered in the process. A new trend, however, is becoming apparent: the whole of many a station area, the right-of-way, passenger station, sidings and approach road, together with any earthworks, is being levelled and submerged under houses and gardens or an industrial estate.

Underbridges (ie rail over road) are disappearing fast and the approach embankments of the former railway are being cut back. Road improvements are also eliminating overbridges (ie road over rail) and these are more difficult to locate. Tunnels appear to be the most likely engineering features to remain.

Not only are stretches of right-of-way which are on the level with the surrounding country being taken into fields and gardens, but embankments are being levelled and cuttings filled. The comparatively low cost of moving earth is not only scarring the countryside with motorways, but is also eliminating traces of former railways to an extent unthought of a few years ago.

All this means that the possibility of walking old railways was diminishing even as these lines were being written. Many planning authorities in South Eastern England have lost a great opportunity to ensure the continuity of the rights-of-way for pedestrian ways or bridle paths. Many miles of old railways run through magnificent scenery in areas where roads are overcrowded and unsafe for pedestrians or riders. However 'The Downs Link' (p82) is the only long-distance footpath. Though a section of the East Grinstead–Groombridge line is part of 'The Forest Way' (p 67), East Sussex County Council has relinquished on the grounds of expense the Culver Junction–Uckfield right-of-way, as has Wealden District Council with their eleven mile 'Cuckoo Walk' (along the Cuckoo Line). Kent County Council has totally neglected the opportunity.

While the visitor to forgotten railways must look for the more obvious remains such as earthworks, other civil engineering features, and buildings, he must also rely on less obvious traces such as property boundaries and railway-type fencing, like the Southern Railway concrete posts and wire, or the pre-Grouping wood or iron fences. Other points to look for are street names. 'Station Road' tends to survive long after the station has been closed. 'Railway Hill' still exists at Barham, 'Halt Stores' is a shop at the site of South Street Halt on the former Canterbury & Whitstable, while their new owners tend to name old railway houses 'The Crossing' or 'The Signal'. At Newick & Chailey the whole station area has become a housing estate, and the adjacent cutting to the bridge carrying the nearby A272 road has been filled in. The only clue to its existence is the road off the A272 which is called Lower Station Road and, 150yd down it, in a front garden, an SR cast-iron notice (presumably at the entrance to the station forecourt) indicating it was a private road.

The visitor must depend on maps. The 50,000 scale is essential (or better still, copies of the old 63,360 series with the lines and stations still marked), but for really detailed work maps on the 25,000 scale or even 10,560 (6in) are necessary. The former shows field boundaries, but the latter shows all property boundaries.

It is not very practicable to walk the lines for any long distance, as considerable diversions are needed. The very best way is to visit the sites by car. Many interesting sites are within easy reach of railway stations, and services on the Southern are still of reasonable frequency. Bus services are still comprehensive, but frequencies are rapidly being reduced. It must be faced that planning itineraries by public transport is becoming more difficult. A combination of rail and cycle is possible, but one difficulty is that the lines are scattered.

The lines have been grouped in geographical order from east to west. Under 'Ownership' it has not been thought necessary to give further details, as after 1922 this is (where appropriate) common in all cases, *viz* Southern Railway, 1 January 1923; British Transport Commission, 1 January 1948; British Railways Board, 1 January 1963. The abbreviations (*pass*) and (*gds*) refer respectively to passenger and freight services. Locations marked * are of particular interest, and are pointed out for the benefit of those whose time for visits may be limited or curtailed.

GROUP 1—EAST KENT

EAST KENT LIGHT RAILWAYS 13¾ miles

ACT: Light Railway Order, 19 June 1911. Subsequent Orders for extensions.

OWNERSHIP: East Kent Light Railways; 1 January 1948, BTC.

OPENED: Shepherd's Well–Wingham Colliery (*gds*), November 1912; (*pass*), 16 October 1916; Eastry–Richborough (*gds*), 1916; Eastry–Sandwich Road (*pass*), 1925; Wingham Colliery–Canterbury Road, 1925.

CLOSED: Eastry–Sandwich Road (*pass*), 31 October 1928; Shepherd's Well–Canterbury Road (*pass*), 30 October 1948; Eastry–Richborough (*gds*), 27 October 1949; Eastry–Canterbury Road (*gds*), 25 July 1950; Eythorne–Eastry (*gds*), 1 July 1951.

SETTING: The 1¾ miles Shepherd's Well–Eythorne–Tilmanstone Colliery unused since 1 March 1984 (miners' strike). Its future is uncertain. Shepherd's Well–Eastry through rolling chalk downland, Eastry–Wingham and Eastry–Sandwich Road through low-lying and intensively farmed land, Sandwich Road–Richborough across coastal marshes and through an industrial area. No station buildings extant. North of Eastry earthworks were few; much right-of-way has been ploughed over. It is only possible to walk a few isolated stretches.

REMAINS

MAIN LINE

Shepherd's Well:* site of EK station (258484) approached by path on BR property to right just inside gate to goods yard. Sidings still in situ. Access to main line over original spur. Cutting for later spur to north. *Golgotha Hill Tunnel* (500yd) (266488) with deep approach cuttings. *Eythorne*: at level crossing (281495) site of station south west of road, junction of branch to Tilmanstone Colliery and main line to north east. Guilford branch trailed in by level crossing to just north east of main line level crossing. *Elvington*: site of halt (formerly Tilmanstone Colliery Halt) (285505) on footpath from Elvington Colliery village to Colliery. Tilmanstone branch rejoined (286513) at level crossing over private road to New Purchase Farm. *Knowlton*: site of halt and level crossing at crossroads (289524). Track parallels Eastry Road and can be easily traced. *Eastry*: site of Eastry South station, south of level crossing on Heronden Lane (301544), site of Eastry Town station (304552) south of Hammil Road, embankment and approach road partially levelled and used as farm yard. Embankment to north, including junction with

Richborough branch still remaining. *Hammil Colliery*: (294558) now a brick-works. Mine offices and other buildings recognisable. No trace of branch connecting colliery with main line. *Woodnesborough*: site of station (298564) to north-west of where road from Woodnesborough to Hammil was crossed. A cutting visible south-east of road, but otherwise from Eastry onwards almost all trace of right-of-way has disappeared, having been taken into the large ploughed fields. *Ash*: site of Ash Town station (286581) on footpath from near Ash church. *Staple*: site of station (275576) difficult to find, but near bridge over small stream. No trace of Staple branch. *Wingham*: site of colliery (250572) now Dambridge Farm. No trace of Wingham Colliery station (252571). Embankment visible between station and level crossing and Wingham Engineering Works (257571). Site of Wingham Town station (245572) now a footpath between Goodnestone and Adisham roads. Site of locomotive siding west of Adisham Road, trains proceeding by gravity to Canterbury Road station (237573) on north side of A257. No trace of station or earthworks on north side but track traceable on south side.

GUILFORD BRANCH

Eythorne: site of junction (281495). *Coldred*: bridge in Church Road (272472) over deep cutting. *Guilford Colliery*: (261468) original buildings including winding-engine house visible in farm yard.

RICHBOROUGH BRANCH

Eastry: site of junction (304552). Embankment visible to *Poison Cross*: site of halt in nursery (309556). Little trace of right-of-way beyond. Site of *Roman Road Halt* (317574) south of level crossing. Faint traces of line to north. Site of *Sandwich Road Halt* (317587) south of A257. *Richborough*: * viaduct over Sandwich–Minster railway (323596), brick piers and approach embankments. No trace of bridge over River Stour but embankment beyond. Site of level crossing (and *Richborough Port Halt* which was never opened to *pass*) on A256 (334601). Traces of line to west of road. To east of level crossing lines went on to quay, behind which Pfizer's factory is now sited. Port lines made end-on junction with SECR siding now used for access to power station. But much has been destroyed by road widening and the arrival of depots for imported cars.

THE THANET LINES

These are the former SER and LCDR lines which became redundant when the two systems in Thanet were linked by the new connecting line opened by the SR on 2 July 1926. They are in two clearly defined sections and are so described here. The sites of *Margate* LCDR, the present Margate station, and *Margate Sands* (SER) are only 200yd apart and those of *Ramsgate Harbour* LCDR and *Ramsgate Town* (SER) only ¾ mile apart. A visit to the lines can therefore be easily done as a round trip, starting from either Margate or Ramsgate.

MARGATE–RAMSGATE HARBOUR abandoned section 1 mile

ACT: Herne Bay–Margate, 22–23 Vic. c.116, 1859; Margate–Ramsgate Harbour, 23–24 Vic. c.241, 1861; second station, never opened, at Margate, 1865.

OWNERSHIP: Margate Railway; 1861, Kent Coast Railway; 1871, LCDR.

OPENED: Herne Bay–Ramsgate Harbour, 5 October 1863.

CLOSED: junction with new line—Ramsgate Harbour, 2 July 1926.

SETTING: the cliff-edged plateau of the Isle of Thanet with some open country, but rapidly becoming more built over as Margate, Broadstairs and Ramsgate expand.

REMAINS: *Margate station*: the present station (347706) was completely rebuilt and greatly enlarged in 1926. No trace of small two-platform Kent Coast station, but parcels dock and siding at far end of forecourt preserve alignment of proposed site of the Margate Railway terminus. No trace of second station which was never opened and which became the 'Hall-by-the-sea', site of station and approach now occupied by 'Dreamland'. Site of *Margate East station* (360700) (closed 1953) on east of overbridge. *Ramsgate*: old formation in deep chalk cutting down at 1 in 75 to north portal of 1,638yd tunnel (390665). Can be seen from trains on 1926 line between Broadstairs and Dumpton Park stations, or from overbridge on road to Dumpton Gap. *Harbour station*: * site (388649) occupied by fun-fair. Retaining walls and south portal of tunnel can easily be seen.

RAMSGATE TOWN–MARGATE SANDS 4½ miles

ACT: Ashford–Canterbury West–Ramsgate–Margate, 7–8 Vic. c.25, 1844. *OWNERSHIP*: SER.

OPENED: Canterbury West–Ramsgate Town, 13 April 1846; Ramsgate Town–Margate Sands, 1 December 1846.

CLOSED: Ramsgate Town station and approach line, Ramsgate

Town–Margate Sands, 2 July 1926.

SETTING: as for LCDR line.

REMAINS: *Ramsgate*: the present station (373658), goods yard and carriage sidings date from 1926. Carriage siding along north side Warre Recreation Ground is line of original approach railway to Ramsgate Town station. This continued across what is now Station Approach Road (not then built) to site of Town station (379656) in 'V' between Chatham Street and Station Approach Road. Station built on hillside on partially made ground and retaining wall can be seen from Chatham Street. *Margate Sands branch*—a reversal was needed in the Town station for trains proceeding to Margate. The point of divergence is obliterated by Station Approach Road, and the first part of the line by the west end of Ramsgate station. It can first be traced by property boundaries at Whitehall Road (372661) and Alkeley Road (369666). The area is wholly built over and the line between can only be traced on a large-scale map. The right-of-way is easily traceable behind Margate Road (A256), though much rubbish has been dumped on it. The Westwood Industrial Estate has been built across the formation. North of the estate is a partially filled shallow cutting which can be approached from Nash Road (357692). A high, wooded embankment can be clearly seen east of the road alongside Tivoli Park. To the south is an underbridge over College Road (B2049). On east side of an underbridge to north is a former SER cottage now a public convenience next to a former SER pumping station. *Margate Goods Station* (1926) (352703) on north end of the line now a coach park/ industrial estate which also occupies the 1926 spur from the main line. The line passed under the latter to reach the terminus. *Margate Sands Station* (348706) at corner of road intersection, the site now occupied by a block of flats.

DOVER AND MARTIN MILL 3½ miles

ACT: Dover, St Margaret's & Martin Mill Light Railways Order, 9 August 1909, giving powers to operate passenger trains. Extensions of time given by subsequent Orders up to that of 11 November 1946.

OWNERSHIP: built and operated by S. Pearson & Son, contractors for Admiralty Harbour; 1909, Dover, St Margaret's & Martin Mill Light Railways; subsequently the War Office.

OPENED: in connection with building the Admiralty Harbour begun in 1897. Part of route re-opened during World Wars I and II. Operated by Royal Engineers mainly to deploy rail-mounted artillery.

CLOSED: after completion of harbour works in 1909.

SETTING: ran across plateau of North Downs from Martin Mill station top of 'white cliffs', zig-zagged down these to Eastern Arm of Harbour.

REMAINS: *Martin Mill*: junction with Dover–Deal line (342466) 370yd south of station. Formation can be traced across fields south east of main line. Embankment and underbridge (329447) on Hangman's Lane at Cherrytree Hole. *Guston*: site of overbridge on A258 Dover–Deal road north of Duke of York's School (333436). Some cuttings on 'main line' and branches can be seen from Upper Road (345431).

THE ELHAM VALLEY (FOLKESTONE–CANTERBURY) 17 miles

ACT: Elham Valley Light Railway with powers to build Cheriton Junction–Harbledown Junction, 44–45 Vic. c.132, 1881.

OWNERSHIP: Elham Valley Light Railway; 1884, SER.

OPENED: Cheriton Junction–Barham, 4 July 1887: Barham–Harbledown Junction, 1 July 1889.

CLOSED: temporary closure (*pass*), Lyminge–Harbledown Junction, 2 December 1940 to 7 October 1946, Cheriton Junction–Lyminge, 3 May 1943 to 7 October 1945. Cheriton Junction–Harbledown Junction (*pass*), 16 June 1947; (*gds*), 10 October 1947. The Army ran goods traffic 1940 to 18 February 1945.

SETTING: The line traversed the beautiful Elham Valley through the North Downs with its picturesque villages.* It closely paralleled the B2065 (a far more pleasant route from Folkestone to Canterbury than the A260). Kent County Council regrettably failed to preserve the integrity of the route as a footpath. It is now impossible to walk it for any distance.

REMAINS: The actual start of the branch was just west of *Folkestone West station* (210365). To Cheriton Junction (191367) it paralleled the main line as a third track. It is now the down slow line of the four-track section. *Cheriton Halt* (201366) was to east of underbridge on B2063, the single platform on north side of branch. Site of Cheriton Junction west of overbridge on B2604,. where four-track section ends. From here the line traceable as earthworks are heavy (but locally obliterated by the M20). Etchinghill Tunnel (166401) under Teddars Lees Road off B2065. *Lyminge*: station at 165413. Wooden 'clapboard' SER building well preserved and now office, and dwelling for Kent County Council Depot in goods yard. Overbridge immediately south on Nash Hill. *Elham*: site of Ottinge siding (170422) north of overbridge on lane east from B2065. Site of Elham station (179437) south of lane leading east from church. Coal merchant uses goods yard. Platform, but site of building occupied by 'Bourne End'. Stationmaster's house in field. At 185445 the line crossed from east to west of B2065, but the road has been rebuilt and the overbridge eliminated. Site of Wingmore siding (186466) south of overbridge on lane leading west from B2065, short access road to siding from B2065. Line visible on low embankment alongside brook. *Barham*: Railway Hill leads west from main road to Derringstone (205495). No trace of line, under new houses. 1963 housing estate on site of station (205495). Heathfield Way (formerly Station Rd) named after a porter. *Kingston*: underbridge (199510) on lane leading south-west from main road. High embankment to north, levelled to south. No trace of line at overbridge on lane from church (196512), cutting filled-in and houses built over it. *Bishopsbourne*: site of station (185525) north of overbridge. Station now private house, also stationmaster's house. *Bridge*: site of station (173544) to north of road from Bridge to White Hill (fork right at 174544). Station approach by bridge abutment. Station now a private dwelling. High embankment and bridge to south. *Canterbury*: site of South station (153565). Hospital built over line to east. Station and line to west can be traced behind houses in South Canterbury Road. Line crossed Wincheap by underbridge at junction of Wincheap and Hollow Lane (141569). Site of Harbledown Junction (137573) with SER Ashford–Canterbury line immediately south-west of LCDR Faversham–Canterbury bridge.

CANTERBURY & WHITSTABLE 6 miles

ACT: 10 June 1825.

OWNERSHIP: Canterbury & Whitstable Railway; 1844, SER.

OPENED: (*formal*) 3 May 1830. Temporary re-opening for coal traffic to Whitstable after floods of January 1953 until Faversham–Whitstable line repaired.

CLOSED: (*pass*) 1 January 1931: (*gds*) 1 December 1952.

SETTING: The route climbs out of the Stour Valley through new suburbs of Canterbury, crosses the wooded plateau of the Blean and drops first through farmland then through Whitstable to the harbour. Much of the right-of-way has been built over or taken-in for cultivation. Only short stretches can be walked, mostly through Blean Forest.

REMAINS: *Canterbury*: site of C&W station (147583) is gateway to goods yard on north-west side of North Lane, 300yd from Westgate Towers. Sidings in coal yard preserve original line of track. Inside gate to right, delapidated building c.1843, originally an office and dwelling. Behind, an equally delapidated stable, similar date. West station (245583),* original 1846 building on up side, a long single-storey stucco building with classical portico. Whitstable trains used short bay at north end of down platform. Line curved sharply left on low embankment, with footpath alongside which can be reached from Roper Road, first right beyond level crossing across St Dunstan's Street. Footpath crosses embankment at 144591. Line enters grounds of Christ Church College and south end Tyler Hill Tunnel (1,102yd) (143595) under College buildings. *Tyler Hill*: north end of tunnel (140152) can be approached from footpath leading west from Calais Hill at junction with the Canterbury–Whitstable road. Site of *Tyler Hill Halt* north of site of level crossing (137611). Driveway to 'The Halt' along formation. 'The Halt' converted from engineman's cottage (Tyler Hill Engine), pond for water supply, all not visible from road. *Clowes Wood*: * it is possible to walk along the formation through Forestry Commission plantation. Approach by footpaths west from car park at Gypsy Corner on Whitstable Road. At 124626 site of Clowes Wood Engine can be identified by pond and widening in right-of-way. Just to north SR-type fencing. Formation descends steeply to north through woods. Site of Bogshole Engine (approx 123644) cannot be identified as formation taken into cultivated fields. *Whitstable*: site of South Street Halt (121655) north of former level crossing over side road immediately west of Canterbury–Whitstable road. Note 'The Halt Stores'. Line walkable to Whitstable & Tankerton station. Overbridge of Thanet Way (A299) (119658)—built for double-track. At Whitstable & Tankerton station (113664) line crossed over road and railway at road signs 'The Bridge Approach', 'Old Bridge Rd'. Site of bridge over Teynham Road (115665). *Harbour*: * site of 1894 station south of level crossing and behind fire station. Tracks crossed road and entered harbour, where they divided to serve south and east quays of basin. No trace of original station (108670).

GROUP 2—NORTH KENT

FAVERSHAM QUAY 1 mile

ACT: 4 August 1853.

OWNERSHIP: East Kent Railway; 1 August 1859, EKR absorbed into LCDR.

OPENED: 12 April 1860.

CLOSED: between 1962 and 1966.

SETTING: through outskirts of Faversham to shore of Faversham Creek.

REMAINS: junction with main line in goods yard east of Faversham station. Rails in situ past disused goods shed, on bridge over Faversham–Goodnestone road (B2040) as far as 024617. Access along lane leading north from B2040 immediately east of railway bridge. Faversham Quay* at far end of Abbey Street, terminus of line was at 022620. Served large warehouse lettered 'United Fertiliser' and 'HB Transport'. Some sleepers in situ.

SHEPPEY LIGHT RAILWAY (QUEENBOROUGH–LEYSDOWN) 8¾ miles

ACT: Light Railway Order, 3 April 1899.

OWNERSHIP: Sheppey Light Railway; 1905, LCDR.

OPENED: Queenborough–Leysdown, 1 August 1901.

CLOSED: Queenborough–Leysdown, 4 December 1950.

SETTING: The line traversed the length of the Isle of Sheppey, an area of low rolling hills and wide marshlands. Agriculture is giving way to industry in the western parts and to bungalows, caravans and holiday chalets elsewhere. Ironically, most of the development has occurred since the line was closed. The line was a surface one and earthworks and structures minimal. Tracing the line is difficult and large-scale maps are essential.

REMAINS: *Queenborough*: main line station (914721).* Remains of Sheppey Light Railway bay behind up platform. Formation visible curving north-east across marshes. Indirect connection with main line at north end of station. *Minster*: site of Sheerness East station (931734) east side of A249 650yd north of traffic lights at Halfway Houses and immediately north of St Katharine Road. Now a yard for lorries. Formation to west of road built over. Site of level crossing across Scrapsgate Road (942729) leading north from B2008. To west track used for farm access, to east taken-in for gardens of houses in Noreen Avenue. Site of *East Minster-on-Sea station* (946727), no trace of station behind shops at corner of B2008 and The Broadway. Line crossed B2008 by level crossing at angle north-west/south-east and continued behind restaurant on south side of road. Site of *Minster-on-Sea station* (954725) and level crossing across Scoles Road. No trace, except rough patch of ground to east. Site of *Brambledown Halt* (963715) very difficult to locate. On south of A250 a belt of trees marks line. On north side, fence between

'Sunfield' and bungalow next door to west marks line of railway, the new bungalow being built on site of the halt. *Eastchurch*: site of station (984704) to west of Church Road just before entrance to HM Prison. New buildings on site of goods yard; tangle of bramble marks platform. Line used as footpath to east. *Leysdown*: site of Harty Road Halt (008705) to east of level crossing across A250 just at corner of Harty Ferry Road. Level crossing over Mustards Road (018005). To east, line built over by holiday camps. Site of station (033707) the car park to east of The Promenade. This preserves shape of passenger station and goods yard layout.

QUEENBOROUGH PIER 1,300yd

ACT: 17 August 1857. *OWNERSHIP*: LCDR.
OPENED: 15 May 1876.
CLOSED: November 1914. Temporary re-opening in 1923 when Kingsferry Bridge was out of action.
SETTING: While in Queenborough take the opportunity of visiting the pier. The Sheerness branch is now very busy with passengers and goods and there are several important private sidings including those to steelworks and docks.
REMAINS: junction with main line 500yd north of *Queenborough station* (913725). First part now a siding used for loading cars. Site of level crossing across B2007 (908729) clearly marked by line to east. To west, line built over by new factory. The pier* (904739) can be reached along foreshore from ancient High Street. Originally T-shaped, the first section of the pier remains and the foundations of the rest can be seen at low tide adjacent to deep water.

STROOD–CHATHAM CENTRAL 1 mile

ACT: 1888.
OWNERSHIP: SER.
OPENED: Strood–Rochester Common (*pass*), 20 July 1891; Rochester Common–Chatham Central (*pass*), 1 March 1892.
CLOSED: Strood–Chatham Central (*pass*), 1 October 1911.
SETTING: A very short (and useless) branch exactly paralleling an existing line through a closely built-up and highly industrialised area of the Medway Towns.
REMAINS:* *Strood*: present station (rebuilt by BRB) (741694). Immediately to south, curve diverges sharply to east from the line to Maidstone West and climbs to join the Victoria–Gillingham line, which crosses over the Maidstone line. This curve is part of the Chatham Central branch (1891)

and it paralleled the original 'Toomer Loop' (1858) which was immediately to the south, and which was eliminated in 1927 by the re-alignment of the line from Victoria to ease the still-severe curve at the foot of Sole Street Bank. Rail bridge over Medway also that of Chatham Central branch, the Victoria line having been diverted on to it in 1927. Eastbound road bridge on line of original LCDR bridge. *Rochester*: Gas House Road (turning north—towards river from The Common) (744686). Immediately beyond present viaduct remains of Chatham Central viaduct, with arches still in use as Kent County Council Estates Department depot. To west, viaduct can be seen as it merges into existing one on the approach to the Medway bridge. To east, embankment in use as shunting neck from Chatham goods depot. The very end of the neck is the site of *Rochester Common station*. Two hundred yards east of junction between Common and Gas House Road, Blue Boar Lane leads under BR viaduct towards river; Chatham Central bridge abutments immediately beyond. Footbridge over Chatham goods depot gives good view of alignment of Chatham Central branch to west. Just west of Rochester station, Funnels Road leads to river under BR viaduct, and brickwork of Chatham Central bridge abutments immediately beyond. Rochester station (748682) was opened 1892 and rebuilt 1912, when original two through platforms were replaced by two island platforms and four tracks. To allow for this enlargement the right-of-way of the Chatham Central branch was built over. East of station BR line to Gillingham crosses over High Street. East of bridge is site of *Chatham Central station* on north side of High Street. By 1974, completely demolished except for outer wall of station-master's house, but in 1986 possible to trace extent of station and yard by property boundaries. Note that station was in Rochester and boundary with Chatham was 400yd east.

CHATTENDEN & UPNOR LIGHT RAILWAY approx 3 miles

ACT: None. *OWNERSHIP*: War Department; 1904, Admiralty.

OPENED: Built for army training purposes 1898. Admiralty operated the line as an inter-depot line, with workmen's services as well as freight. Never a public railway.

CLOSED: 31 December 1961 (last scheduled service 19 May 1961).

GAUGE: 2ft 6in (76cm).

SETTING: The line ran from just south of the old village of Upnor on the bank of the Medway, round the prominent Beacon Hill to the Ministry of Defence establishments north of the A228 road to Grain.

REMAINS: *Upnor*: at 757706 a new road* (owned by the Ministry of Defence but normally open to the public) leads north on the north side of Upnor Road at a sharp bend in the latter just before Upnor High Street. The new road closely parallels the C&U formation, which can be seen as a low embankment just to the west. South of Upnor Road no further trace of line to terminus at Tower Hill Camp, Upper Upnor (757702). At the Church (757710) the new road crosses Lower Upnor Road. Cutting for new road has destroyed site of the junction of 'main line' with Lower Upnor branch just to the north of Lower Upnor Road, while south of latter and on to Lower Upnor there is no trace of the branch. New road (now Upchat Road)* continues on line of C&U round base of Beacon Hill to 754714 where it diverges to the west to cross over A228 by a new bridge. Two hundred yards east can be seen C&U embankment on either side of site of the railway bridge. At roundabout (755720) new road to north (not open to public) continues on line of C&U behind the barracks. From roundabout Chattenden Lane can be gained and followed north to where it is joined by the private road at the point where the C&U probably entered Lodge Hill Ammunition Depot at 756733.

CHATTENDEN NAVAL TRAMWAY–KINGSNORTH LIGHT RAILWAY 4¼ miles

ACT: Chattenden Naval Tramways Order, 1901 authorising line from Lodge Hill to Kingsnorth; Kingsnorth Light Railway Order (permitting passenger service east of Sharnal Street), 6 November 1926; Kingsnorth Light Railway Order (transferring ownership east of Sharnal Street), 25 July 1929.

OWNERSHIP: Admiralty; 1919, section east of Sharnal Street leased by Kingsnorth Light Railway Co; 1929, ownership of that section assumed by Kingsnorth Light Railway.

OPENED: Lodge Hill–Sharnal Street (goods, Admiralty traffic only), 1901; Sharnal Street–Kingsnorth Pier (goods, Admiralty traffic), 1915.

CLOSED: Sharnal Street–Kingsnorth, date unknown but between 1945 and 1957; Lodge Hill–Sharnal Street, probably 1961, but traffic always very sparse and irregular.

SETTING: The line traversed a wide valley in the rolling countryside of the Hoo Peninsula from Lodge Hill Depot down to the lonely Sharnal Street station and across the marshes to the shore of the Medway Estuary.

REMAINS: *Lodge Hill Depot*: within which was the terminus of the line, lies west of overbridge at Lower Deangate (773739).

Formation clearly visible along floor of valley to *Sharnal Street* (788743),* where former station approach runs between formation of light railway and BR line. Separate arch at overbridge on A228. Site of exchange sidings east of bridge. *Beluncle Farm*: overbridge on road 300yd east of farm on old section of Stoke Road just north of present road (802735). Filled-in cutting. To south-east formation obliterated by an orchard. Beyond again line built over by former Berry Wiggins oil refinery and by Kingsnorth Power Station.

HOO JUNCTION–PORT VICTORIA 12½ miles

ACT: Hoo Junction–Stoke, 42–43 Vic. c.126, 1879; Stoke–Port Victoria, 43–44 Vic. c.117, 1880.

OWNERSHIP: Hundred of Hoo Railway Co; 1881, SER.

OPENED: Hoo Junction–Sharnal Street, 1 April 1882; Sharnal Street–Port Victoria, 11 September 1882.

CLOSED: Grain–Port Victoria (*pass*), 4 September 1951; Hoo Junction–Grain (*pass*), 4 December 1961.

SETTING: The Hundred of Hoo, a peninsula between Thames and Lower Medway is an area of fascinating contrasts. Low-lying, but with wide views, agricultural but with modern industry, old villages with ancient churches surrounded by new estates and caravan sites, shipping on both rivers. Strictly speaking, the line is not forgotten: sea-dredged aggregates are railed from a siding built to serve a cement plant, closed when production was concentrated on Northfleet in 1970. In 1982 Grain refinery closed, but refined products are landed and some railed. A 1986 visit showed the rails had a 'used' look. The line is worth including in a tour of the other forgotten railways in the Hundred of Hoo in order to see traces of former stations which were the life-line of what was, before the motor-age, an area of great isolation. Dickens' famous novel, 'Great Expectations' had Cooling as background.

REMAINS: *Hoo Junction*: junction of Hundred of Hoo branch with electrified Gravesend–Strood line (699735). Marshalling yard in use but of less importance than formerly. Site of Uralite Halt (701737) approached only by footpath from King's Farm (703730) as it served Uralite Works adjacent on north side of line, which also had a private siding. *Cliffe*:* siding to Brett Marine aggregate loading point (721745). Site of Cliffe station east of overbridge on B2000 (737748) with station approach. Mile and a quarter to village centre. *High Halstow*: site of High Halstow Halt and Wybourne Siding (773751) on west of level crossing over track from Cooling

Road (450yd west of church) to Wybourne Farm. *Hoo St Werburgh*: site of Sharnal Street station* (788743), 1¾ miles from Hoo St Werburgh and two miles from Hoo St Mary. Site best seen from overbridge on A228. *Note*: (1) course of Chattenden Naval Tramway as field boundaries curving south-east; (2) site of exchange sidings east of second overbridge; (3) electricity sub-station on site of station buildings, remains of up platform; (4) isolated site of station. Site of Beluncle Halt and Siding (803737) east of Stoke Road. Private siding to former Barry Wiggins refinery (812738) now an industrial estate. *Stoke*: site of Middle Stoke Halt (833752) on track from A228 (on sharp bend at Court Farm) down to shore. Remains of Stoke Junction Halt and site of siding west of level crossing over A228 (843756). Site of junction with Allhallows branch 130yd east of level crossing. *Grain*: * site of Grain Crossing Halt (863753) at signal box controlling level crossing at point where A228 becomes B2001 and entrance to rail system of former refinery. Platform of Grain station (868749) alongside B2001 at bend. Road continues to Grain village. It is not possible to reach the site of Port Victoria Pier (878739) through the tank farm, though rails are laid to within 200yd. Little trace of Yantlet Wharf branch.

STOKE JUNCTION–ALLHALLOWS-ON-SEA 1¾ miles

ACT: Light Railway Order, June 1929.

OWNERSHIP: Southern Railway.

OPENED: 14 May 1932. Doubled 1935. Singled 1957.

CLOSED: 4 December 1961.

SETTING: Across bleak coastal marshes to the foot of the low hill on which Allhallows is built. It must be remembered that, apart from the old village centre of Hoo Allhallows, virtually all building is post-1945.

REMAINS: Site of Stoke Junction with Port Victoria line (844756) 130yd east of level crossing over A228. Formation can be easily traced over marshes by fencing, but difficult to walk, as some bridges over drains have been removed. *Allhallows-on-Sea*: site of station (884783), goods yard and first part of right-of-way occupied by Kingsmead Residential Caravan Site. Note 'British Pilot' inn and 'Albany Court' (flats)–only buildings near station erected by estate company before 1939. Road up hill from station built by company in connection with railway.

FAWKHAM JUNCTION–GRAVESEND WEST 5 miles

ACT: 18 July 1881; pier at Gravesend and extension thereto, 24 July 1882.

OWNERSHIP: Gravesend Railway Co; 1883, LCDR.
OPENED: Fawkham Junction–Gravesend (*formal*), 17 April 1886, (*pass* & *gds*), 10 May 1886.
CLOSED: Fawkham Junction–Gravesend West (*pass*), 3 August 1953; Southfleet–Gravesend West (*gds*), 24 March 1968.
SETTING: South of A2 line runs through rising ground intensively cultivated for market gardens, so earthworks are easily seen. Northward formation can be traced through the built-up area of Gravesend. Single line of rails, overgrown, as far as bridge over Dartford–Gravesend line.
REMAINS: *Longfield*: Fawkham Junction (593692), junction of Gravesend branch with main line. Can be reached by footpath from lane to Pinden 150yd south of junction with B260. Site of Longfield Halt south-west of overbridge at 599698. *Southfleet*: site of station north of overbridge on Station Road (B262) (614720). A second line of rails at this point reveals the outline of the former island platform. In 1974 the goods yard to the north became a coal concentration point for APCM cement plants in Gravesend area. Now no longer in use. Line was used as shunting neck as far as modern bridge over A2. Beyond line in situ to 632735. *Gravesend*: site of Perry Street sidings north of overbridge on Dover Road East (632736). Site of Rosherville station (644741), station approach leads south from London Road opposite Pier Road. Gravesend West station (644743) delapidated but almost untouched. Pier extension can be easily seen, the platform is on the bridge over West Street. Goods yard above the station entrance a car park. Goods shed still there. *Note*: while in Gravesend a visit to the Town Pier at the end of the High Street (648745) is worthwhile. The former London, Tilbury & Southend 'station' still survives. It had all the usual offices and facilities, but once through the ticket barrier a ramp led down not to a platform and trains but to a landing stage and ferries to Tilbury Riverside station.

GROUP 3—MID-KENT AND ROMNEY MARSH

SANDLING–SANDGATE $3\frac{1}{2}$ miles

ACT: 27–28 Vic. c.99, 1864; powers to extend to Folkestone Harbour, 39–40 Vic. c.228, 1876.
OWNERSHIP: SER.
OPENED: Sandling–Sandgate, 9 October 1874; reopened (*pass*), Sandling–Hythe, 1945.
CLOSED: Hythe–Sandgate, 1 April 1931; Sandling–Hythe (*pass*), 1943; Sandling–Hythe, 3 December 1951.

SETTING: The area is very hilly and the branch involved heavy earthworks. It can be easily traced and walked in large part nearly to Hythe. Beyond Hythe it is fast disappearing under bulldozers preparing for housing development and a 6in map is necessary to trace it. On the last bit before Sandgate contrasts can be drawn between these modern methods and 1930s houses incredibly perched on embankments. A visit to the branch should be coupled with one to the still much used Folkestone Harbour station and the incline down from Folkestone Junction paralleled by a street called 'the Tram Road'.

REMAINS: *Sandling*: main line station (148368),* 'cottage' type building on up platform (similar to style of Folkestone Central before rebuilding), down branch platform (up branch platform has disappeared), single-track siding on branch right-of-way. *Saltwood*: overbridge on Grange Road (past the castle) (160362). Between Sandling and this point heavy earthworks, including 100yd tunnel (153365), survive and it is possible to walk the track. *Hythe*: site of station (167353) now being built over just below junction of Cannongate Road and Cliff Road on west of former. Station approach leads down to crossroads and on into town by Station Road. Two hundred yards east along Cliff Road overlooks site of goods yard now being built over. At 179351 is Cliff Road overbridge, beyond which line can be traced in cutting for 100yd. *Sandgate*: Horn Street (B2604) underbridge (186351), turn west into Naildown Road immediately north of bridge; the houses on south side are built on the embankment of the branch. Further up Naildown Road, Naildown Close is also built over the line. At entrance to the Close a good view to east of line to Sandgate station and how it has been built over.* Return to corner of Horn Street and Seabrook Road and ascend Hospital Hill (B2063). Houses on south side built on embankment of line. Bus garage (188350) built over line at entrance to station. Site of station and remains of platform with wreckage of 'Gents' visible from Hospital Road beyond garage. Return to Seabrook Road and where this leaves the Esplanade (190349), station approach leads upward.

APPLEDORE–DUNGENESS / NEW ROMNEY 11⅓ miles
branch 4¼ miles

ACT: 36–37 Vic. c.234, 1873, incorporating Rye & Dungeness Pier Co; 38–39 Vic. c.181, 1875, powers transferred to SER; 44–45 Vic. c.5, 1881, incorporating Lydd Railway Co, with powers to build Appledore–Dungeness; 45–46 Vic. c.155, 1882, New Romney branch.

OWNERSHIP: Lydd Railway: 1895, SER.

OPENED: Appledore–Dungeness (*gds*), 7 December 1881: Appledore–Lydd Town (*pass*), 7 December 1881: Lydd Town–Dungeness (*pass*), 19 June 1884: Romney Junction–New Romney, 19 June 1884; re-aligned Romney (New) Junction–New Romney, 4 July 1937.

CLOSED: Romney (New) Junction (milepost 74)–Dungeness (*pass*), 4 July 1937,(*gds*), May 1953; Appledore–New Romney (*pass*), 6 March 1967: Romney (New) Junction–New Romney (*gds*), 6 March 1967.

SETTING: The line is still in use from the lonely station at Appledore to milepost 74. Here atomic waste is railed, while block trains of aggregate are loaded at milepost 73. The whole line is level throughout. From Appledore to Lydd Town it traverses the intensively farmed Romney Marsh. Beyond Lydd it crosses the shingle spread of Dungeness. Holiday bungalows sprawl along the shore and inland to the line of the old railway. Here both the older and the newer alignments can easily be traced, though walking on the shingle is hard and tiring.

REMAINS: *Appledore*: when the area was visited in 1974 the Ashford–Ore line had been under threat of closure to passengers for many years, but this was lifted after the Ministerial announcement of 31 July 1974. Appledore station* is worth a visit as an example of an SER roadside station which has survived almost unaltered. The junction is 200yd south. From here to milepost 74 (076191) the single track is in situ. *Brookland*: site of station at 997264. Station building on down platform in use as dwelling, up platform visible. *Lydd*: Town station (050216),* station buildings, passing loop, platforms and five-siding goods yard remain as a complete SER country station. No trace of Army-owned system linking goods yard with the artillery ranges. Site of Romney (Old) Junction (061207). Siding for aggregate loading (068202). Romney (New) Junction (076191), now loading point for atomic waste, two short sidings, one aligned along Dungeness line, the other along New Romney branch. Access road to atomic power station now occupies line south from former level crossing. *Dungeness*: short platform (088170) 50yd west of RHDR station. *Lydd-on-Sea station*: (084191) forecourt and island platform, approach road built by SR. *Greatstone-on-Sea station*: (076225) at end of SR-built approach road past St Peter's Church. Forecourt and platform remain. *New Romney*: junction of old and new alignments (071237), site of station

(074248) now an industrial estate. Site of siding to RHDR occupied by west part of new covered RHDR station. A visit to Marine Parade, Littlestone* is well worth while, to see the Victorian blocks of houses and hotels, remains of the first attempt to create a seaside resort.

RYE AND CAMBER 2½ miles

ACT: None. *OWNERSHIP*: Rye & Camber Tramways Co.

OPENED: Rye–Camber Golf Links (*pass*), 13 July 1895; Camber Golf Links–Camber Sands (*pass*), 13 July 1908. In partial use 1939–46 by War Office.

GAUGE: 3ft 0in.

CLOSED: Rye–Camber Sands (*pass*), September 1939.

SETTING: From the foot of the hill on which Rye is built across the coastal flats to the mouth of the Rother.

REMAINS: Site of Rye terminus on south side of A259 Rye–New Romney Road just across bridge over River Rother (925206). Formation can be traced as footpath as far as site of bridge over creek at 931203. At Rye Harbour on far side of River Rother at the ferry, the corrugated-iron building of Camber Golf Links station survives as office of M. J. Haynes–Boat Hire (935192). Rails embedded in concrete outside station. Road leading west built by army along right-of-way. At 952188, site of Camber Sands station can be distinguished among dunes 400yd south of Camber Road.

RYE HARBOUR 2 miles

ACT: 18 June 1846 (8 & 9 Vic C55). *OWNERSHIP*: SER.

OPENED: (*gds*), March 1854. *CLOSED*: after 1962.

SETTING: Across the coastal flats below Rye town to Rye Harbour at the mouth of the Rother.

REMAINS: Junction with Ashford–Hastings line at 916202. The branch trailed in to down (to Hastings) line south of bridge over River Tillingham. Site of level crossing (919199) across A259 Rye–Winchelsea Road just north of Martello tower. Site of bridge across River Brede (920198). Formation can be traced to south of Harbour Road. At 931194 private siding crossed road to enter Rye Oil Refinery. At 935193 level crossing of branch across Harbour Road. Private siding continued on to Rye Spun Concrete works. At Rye Harbour village the terminus of the branch and the formation approaching it can be seen on bank of river just above the slipway (942191). Originally the line ended on a short wooden pier. There appears to be no space for loop or sidings.

KENT & EAST SUSSEX (ROBERTSBRIDGE–HEADCORN) 21½ miles

ACT: Light Railway Order 1896, incorporating Rother Valley (Light) Railway, authorisation Robertsbridge–Tenterden; Order 1903, Headcorn Extension; Order 1904, company title altered to Kent & East Sussex Light Railway; Order 1973, transfer of ownership and authorisation to re-open.

OWNERSHIP: Rother Valley (Light) Railway; 1904 Kent & East Sussex Light Railway; 1948, BTC; Rother Valley Light Railway—between Tenterden Town and Bodiam inclusive.

OPENED: Robertsbridge–Rolvenden (*gds*), 29 March 1900, (*pass*), 2 April 1900; Rolvenden–Tenterden Town, 15 April 1903; Tenterden Town–Headcorn, 15 May 1905. Re-opened: Tenterden Town–Rolvenden (*pass*) 3 February 1974; Rolvenden–Newmill Bridge, 1975; Newmill Bridge–Wittersham Rd, 1978.

CLOSED: Robertsbridge–Headcorn (*pass*), 4 January 1954: Tenterden Town–Headcorn (*gds*), 4 January 1954; after closure to regular passenger traffic, hop-pickers' specials ran during the season until the end of 1959; Robertsbridge–Tenterden Town (*gds*), 12 June 1961.

SETTING: Between Robertsbridge and Rolvenden the line keeps to the Rother Valley and the Newmill Channel through low-lying grazing land (reclaimed from marsh), with low hills on either side. From Rolvenden to Tenterden Town the line climbs steeply into the Weald to run across the plateau to Biddenden and descend gently thence to Headcorn. All the villages it served as well as Tenterden itself are well worth visiting. The line can be walked for much of the way between Robertsbridge and Bodiam. From here to Tenterden Town it has been preserved and is gradually being brought back into use. In 1986 trains were running to Hexden Bridge (857278). The northern stretch has been largely taken into farmland and it is no longer possible to walk it.

REMAINS: *Robertsbridge*: Italianate main line station (733235).* Short bay at north end of down platform was used by K&ESR trains. Site of junction 100yd north. Level crossing across A21 (738240). Private siding into Pride of Sussex flour mill trailed in just to east and had its own level crossing. *Salehurst*: site of halt (751241) on footpath south from church. In this part, line can easily be walked. *Junction Road*: site of halt on east side of level crossing across A229 (The Junction Road) (771243). Short shelterless platform in situ, though siding removed. *Bodiam*: station west of level crossing (784250).

From here on the line definitely not a forgotten one and is in process of restoration, but is still well worth visiting.* *Northiam*: station west of level crossing (835265). Like all K&ESR stations except Tenterden Town, a simple wooden frame, corrugated-iron clad building. Also in yard two K&ESR houses, single-storey wooden ones. *Wittersham*: Wittersham Road station north-east of level crossing on lane from Wittersham to Rolvenden (866287). Station building removed, but signal box erected and sidings laid. *Rolvenden*: station south of level crossing on A28 (864328). Main depot of line. *Tenterden*: Town station* well signposted and at end of Station Road (882335). Well-preserved simple brick-and-timber building and headquarters of the line. Trains run at weekends. Rails continue north to 884341. Site of St Michael's Halt and level crossing south end of Orchard Road (883352). Latter built along right-of-way. St Michael's Tunnel (30yd) (883354) under lane. Cutting to north. Line north of this unwalkable as it is frequently blocked by fences, taken-in to fields, or completely overgrown. *High Halden*: site of High Halden Road station north-west of level crossing on A262 (878367). Small wooden stationmaster's house and station building converted to dwelling. *Biddenden*: site of station and level crossing on B2078 (853392). Wooden stationmaster's house in use. Station converted to dwelling. Goods yard now a garden. *Frittenden*: Frittenden Road (843148), site on north side of lane from Lashenden to Frittenden and nearer Biddenden than Frittenden village! Station very delapidated and overgrown, and line on to Headcorn almost completely obliterated. *Headcorn*: main line station (837440).* K&ESR platform face can be seen on south side of up platform. Formation can be seen curving away to south past milk-factory.

PADDOCK WOOD–HAWKHURST 11½ miles

ACT: Powers to build Paddock Wood–Cranbrook, 8 August 1877; Hawkhurst extension, 12 July 1882.

OWNERSHIP: Cranbrook & Paddock Wood Railway Co; 1882, SER.

OPENED: Paddock Wood–Goudhurst, 1 October 1892; Goudhurst–Hawkhurst, 4 September 1893.

CLOSED: Paddock Wood–Hawkhurst, 12 June 1961.

SETTING: The line ran through most beautiful countryside, well worth visiting for its own sake. It is hilly with numerous orchards, hop gardens and woods. Although heavy earthworks were involved, many have been levelled and much line has been taken-in to fields and orchards. Walking impossible.

REMAINS: *Paddock Wood*: main line station (671453). Original 1842 building on down side demolished. Bay at east end of up platform was the Hawkhurst bay. Siding on branch to approx 676452. Branch, which had paralleled the main line began to diverge at 679452. From here onward most of the right-of-way has been taken-in to the fields, but even so, when the site of the line can be approached by footpath it can in places be traced by property and field boundaries. *Horsmonden*: site of Churn Siding (575428). Tile-hung railway house (now called 'Churn Siding') south-west of level crossing. To north-west, site of line under cultivation. Overbridge (576423) on Crook Road, embankment visible to south. Tunnel (86yd) (573411) under B2162 with approach cuttings. Station (575404) north of road survives as 'Station Garage'. Like all stations on branch, single-storey, wood-frame, corrugated-iron clad. Underbridge on road has disappeared, and few traces left as far as Hope Mill (Goudhurst Station). *Goudhurst*: site of station at Hope Mill (578372) has been completely cleared and a house built approximately on goods yard. South of road the right-of-way has been taken over for $\frac{1}{4}$ mile as a diversion to the drive to Finchcocks House. Pattenden Siding was just east of overbridge (721366). Right-of-way now part of a new orchard to west. Traces of cuttings and embankments through Furnace Wood. *Cranbrook*: long approach road from Railway Hotel on A229 at Hartley (757345) to station (754345). Station* now in very poor condition, stationmaster's house with large dormer-windows now a dwelling. Coal merchant uses goods yard, goods shed survives. Deep cutting to south. *Hawkhurst*: Badger's Oak Tunnel (178yd) (754335). Station (758322)* at Gills Green just west of A229. Whole station area now owned by Kent Woodware Co. Station building demolished, but platform survives. Signal box in good repair and newly painted. Note goods shed, locomotive shed, tile-hung stationmaster's house and row of SER cottages to north.

CROWHURST–BEXHILL WEST $4\frac{1}{3}$ miles

ACT: 15 July 1897.

OWNERSHIP: Crowhurst, Sidley & Bexhill Railway; 1905, SER.

OPENED: 1 June 1902.

CLOSED: 1 January 1917 – 1 March 1919. (Gds) 9 September 1963, (*pass*) 15 June 1964.

SETTING: The line ran through high ground, across a broad valley and down to the coast through the suburbs of Bexhill.

REMAINS: *Crowhurst*: station* (760129) dates from building of branch. In spacious style of SECR (*cf* Chislehurst, Orpington). Track layout has been greatly simplified. Former bays at south end of each platform were used by branch trains. Note the long approach, contemporary with station. Junction 400yd south of station (764128). Cutting at overbridge (763113). Site of 17 arch viaduct* (demolished 1969) (763104). *Bexhill*: site of Sidley station south of overbridge on A270 (742090); site of passenger station now a garage; goods yard a lorry park and council yard. Underbridge on A259. Bexhill West station* now owned by Rother District Council. Former refreshment room operates as the 'Rother Arms'. Light industry on site of goods yard. Station separated only by a road from LBSCR, but never a physical link.

DUNTON GREEN–WESTERHAM 4¾ miles

ACT: 24 July 1876.

OWNERSHIP: Westerham Valley Railway Co; 1881, SER.

OPENED: 7 July 1881. *CLOSED*: 30 October 1961.

SETTING: The line ran along part of the Vale of Holmesdale below the North Downs through very pretty country to the old town of Westerham.

REMAINS: *Dunton Green*: main line station (515575). Site of branch platform and loop can clearly be seen beyond entrance to subway under branch formation. 100yd to west, line taken in to gardens of houses in Leonard Road. Overbridge on Sevenoaks Road (511573) is extant, but cutting filled-in and new school built over right-of-way east of road. *Chipstead*: site of Chevening Halt (495568) 100yd south of bridge over A21(M) on Chevening Road obliterated by a motorway interchange. For 2¼ miles westward to approximately 460554 the right-of-way has been submerged under the M25. *Brasted*: station (467558) has disappeared under M25 but road from Church is Station Road with railway-type street lights. *Westerham*: site of station (448544) on London Road opposite 'The Crown' inn. Forecourt still there and wall-type post box re-set in brick pillar. Site of station and extensive yard taken over by Station Trading Centre. East of station line taken-in to gardens.

GROUP 4—EAST SUSSEX

THREE BRIDGES–GROVE JUNCTION 25¼ miles

ACT: Powers to LBSCR to build Three Bridges–East Grinstead, 18 June 1846; powers to East Grinstead Railway, 8 July 1853; East Grinstead–Grove Junction, 7 August 1862; Birchden

Junction–Groombridge Junction, 1861.

OWNERSHIP: Three Bridges–East Grinstead, East Grinstead Railway; January 1865, LBSCR; East Grinstead–Grove Junction, East Grinstead, Groombridge & Tunbridge Wells Railway; 29 July 1864, LBSCR; Birchden Junction–Groombridge Junction, Brighton, Uckfield & Tunbridge Wells Railway; 29 July 1864, LBSCR.

OPENED: Three Bridges–East Grinstead, 9 July 1855; East Grinstead–Tunbridge Wells West, 1 October 1866; Tunbridge Wells West–Grove Junction, about 1867 (*gds*), 1 February 1876 (*pass*); Birchden Junction–Groombridge Junction, 3 August 1868.

CLOSED: Three Bridges–Groombridge Junction, 2 January 1967. Rowfant petroleum depot continued to be served from Three Bridges until line severed by M23. Birchden Junction–Groombridge–Grove Junction, 7 July 1985.

SETTING: The line ran through very beautiful and surprisingly remote countryside. Crawley New Town, East Grinstead and Tunbridge Wells are the only places of any consequence. The area is heavily wooded, though less so between East Grinstead and Groombridge. East of Forest Row the line ran through the valley of the Upper Medway and its tributaries with particularly attractive villages.

REMAINS: *Three Bridges*: station (288369).* Buildings on down side are original ones and pre-date quadrupling. The covered bay at south end of platform used by the branch trains. Formation can be seen curving sharply to east immediately south of station. Overbridge on B2036 (298365) with cutting to east. M23 has severed the line east of Worth Church at approximately 305366. Former level crossing at 315366. *Rowfant Station** (325368): Tudoresque building in use as a dwelling, goods yard used by chemical company, level crossing with former petroleum depot to west. No village, Rowfant House (326372). To east of station tree-grown embankment with underbridges. *Grange Road*: site of station (346374); buildings and platform removed and yard obliterated for housing. Formation to west in use as footpath; to east under new houses. Quite a large post-railway settlement round station, which has grown since closure: this is Crawley Down (the old nucleus being on B2028). Station named after The Grange (348369). Turner's Hill 1½ miles south along B2028. *East Grinstead*:* overbridge and site of Imberhorne Siding (376382). Site of High Level station (1882) (388383) marked by footbridge over present station (rebuilt Low Level station). From the footbridge is best view of layout. To west, car park on site of divergence of lines to Three Bridges and to St Margaret's Junction (site at 391390). To east, Inner Relief Road (1978) has been built on right-of-way of line to Forest Row. Second station (1886–83) was located in cutting west of bridge under London Road (392383), but bridge eliminated when Relief Road built. Site of upper goods yard also taken over by new road. Between this and Station Approach Road is original station (1855) in use as offices and attractively landscaped. Below footbridge are new station buildings on site of Low Level station (1882). South-east of sidings in former lower goods yard is embankment of former spur to upper goods yard. Note old railway houses in Brooklands Way. Note also shunting neck on Imberhorne Viaduct to south (383373). Railway to Forest Row beyond London Road overbridge skirted town in deep cuttings and short tunnels under College Road and Lewes Road (A22). *Forest Row*: bridge at 425455 over A22 removed with road widening, but embankments on either side remain. Site of station (428352) at end of long approach road from A264, Tunbridge Wells road. Station demolished and site incorporated in Social Club. Fire station and council yard on goods yard site. *Hartfield*: station* (480362) just east of bridge on B2606. In use as private house, goods yard in use by a coal merchant, also goods shed. Formation to west of bridge part of 'Forest Way'. *Withyham*: station (499364) east of former level crossing and now a house, 'White Gables'. Road still called 'Station Road'. Formation part of 'Forest Way'. Line on low embankment and easily traced eastward along valley floor. *Groombridge*: underbridge on B2110 at Ham Bridge (515369) removed, but embankment to site of Ashurst Junction (where line trailed into Oxted–Uckfield line). Groombridge Junction (532368) was site of junction of curves from Ashurst and Birchden Junctions. When the line was visited in September 1985 everything was still in situ. Station a typical LBSC roadside one with three platforms. Site of *High Rocks Halt* (559383). *Tunbridge Wells*: West station (578384) very large gaunt, ugly structure with three platforms. D/EMU depot to south on site of locomotive depôt and goods yard. Site can best be seen from bridge at 581384, from which the tunnel can also be seen. Site of Grove Junction (586387) can only be seen from trains on the Tunbridge Wells Central–Hastings line.

ERIDGE–POLEGATE ('THE CUCKOO LINE') 20½ miles

ACT: Polegate–Hailsham, 7–8 Vic. c.91, 1846; Hailsham–Tunbridge Wells (3ft 0in gauge line); Hailsham–Eridge, 36–37 Vic. c.226, 1873.

OWNERSHIP: Tunbridge Wells & Eastbourne Railway Co; 1876, LBSCR.

OPENED: Polegate–Hailsham, 14 May 1849; Hailsham–Heathfield, 5 April 1880; Heathfield–Eridge, 1 September 1880; Redgate Mill Junction–Eridge incorporated with Uckfield line as double track, 1894.

CLOSED: Heathfield–Redgate Mill Junction, 14 June 1965; Hailsham–Heathfield (*pass*), 14 June 1965; Hailsham–Heathfield (*gds*), 26 April 1968; Polegate–Hailsham, 9 September 1968.

SETTING: From Redgate Mill the line wound through the heavily-wooded Wealden hills with sharp curves and steep grades until south of Hellingly it emerged on to the low-lying clay plain on the edge of Pevensey Levels and with the South Downs away to the south. Here the scenery, though not remarkable, is very pleasant.

REMAINS: *Eridge*: station* (543346) still in use but should be visited. Named after Eridge Park, and the inn is the only building nearby. Formerly an important interchange and many trains split and joined. Originally two island platforms. Note also Birchden Junction at 531356. *Redgate Mill Junction*:* (551326) approached by lane from A26. The line south from Eridge double (originally two single lines). Signal posts in situ. First 330yd of embankment including bridge still in situ. South of bridge, embankment levelled for sewage works. Line can be easily traced up to *Rotherfield* station (566303).* Tile-hung stationmaster's house joined to single-storey station building, standard on the line. House in use as dwelling, station building converted to another dwelling; platform awning converted to sun-lounge and swimming pool constructed between platforms. Underbridge south of station. Line easily traced on and up to *Mayfield* station (578267) converted into dwelling at end of Station Road. Note tunnels under A267 (60yd) (571286) and (70yd) (581278). South of Mayfield some eleven miles became 'The Cuckoo Walk', but unfortunately the local authority, seeking to reduce expenditure, has abandoned it and by 1986 had begun to destroy the integrity of the right-of-way by selling off parcels of land. *Heathfield*: site of station (581213) is best seen from overbridge on road opposite the Heathfield Hotel. To south site of station (the buildings were on the hill behind) and goods yard, which is being taken over as an industrial estate. To north the portal of the tunnel (270yd), in agricultural use. Natural gas container was situated here. Between here and Horham, earthworks and bridges remain and line can be readily approached from B2203.* *Horham*: station (578174) exists complete but unused and very delapidated. Goods yard used by coal merchant. Like Heathfield, village is post-railway. Original name of station was Waldron & Horeham Road. Waldron Church two miles north-west. Horeham Manor on west of A267. *Hellingly*: * station (584120) in use as dwelling. Haulage contractor uses approach and goods yard. Traces may be seen of former electrically-operated goods line to Hellingly Hospital from siding on down side south of station. At crossroads (589119) gate (site level crossing) on road south to Leap Cross with line of hedge to west. Gate on north side of road east to Magham Downs, with low embankment across hospital grounds. *Hailsham*: * overbridge on B2202 at 588098. Site of station at 589093, now occupied by an industrial estate. Note Station Road, stationmaster's house and Terminus Hotel (Hailsham was the terminus 1849–80). Site of level crossing across B2104 at 588077, note keeper's house. Site of private siding (587067) to brickworks (582069). *Polegate*: * overbridge on A27 over 1880 formation (583050). The 1849 formation crossed A27 200yd east; north of road, followed line of Westfield Close; south of road, is a railway-owned footpath. Station of 1880 (586047), a huge toasted-brick erection in use to 1985 when new station opened on site. Site of original station east of level crossing over High Street (582048). Stationmaster's house is seen.

LEWES–UCKFIELD 8½ miles

ACT: 27 July 1856.

OWNERSHIP: Lewes & Uckfield Railway Co; 1859, LBSCR.

OPENED: Uckfield Junction–Uckfield, 18 October 1858; re-alignment Lewes–Hamsey, 1 October 1868. Re-opened 1983 by private owner as 'Lavender Line' for one mile northward from Isfield.

CLOSED: Uckfield Junction–Hamsey, 1 October 1868. Last train Lewes–Uckfield, 23 February 1969. Bus replacement provided by BR until official closure, 6 May 1969.

SETTING: The line ran up the Ouse Valley. At one time it could be walked from Hamsey to Uckfield, but the East Sussex County Council, having failed to secure re-opening, have allowed the right-of-way to be severed in a number of places.

REMAINS: *Lewes*: * site of 1846 station 100yd up Friar's Walk from junction with High Street. Abutments of 1868 line in Cliffe High Street 50yd east of junction with Friar's Walk. Viaduct can be traced across old goods yard to south, and behind buildings on north side of road for 175yd. Beyond, formation destroyed by new inner ring-road. Viaduct across Ouse demolished. Formation can be easily traced north of river. The 1868 line joins 1858 formation at 415127. For 1,300yd westward 1858 line can be traced to site of Uckfield Junction (405115) on Lewes–Keymer Junction line. Formation is farm track west to site of level crossing (411124) with a well-preserved keeper's cottage. Formation taken in to fields west to site of level crossing at 408124, with another keeper's cottage. From here to junction formation is a line of trees. *Barcombe*: site of Culver Junction (426143),* Uckfield and East Grinstead lines diverge north of overbridge on unmade road from Barcombe village. Barcombe Mills station* (420149) in good order, in use as a dwelling, level crossing with rails in situ. North of level crossing notice saying footpath by lineside can be used when road is flooded. *Isfield*: station (453171) very well restored, new depot in goods yard and single line laid to 457184. *Uckfield*: by-pass under construction 1985 crosses approx 468208. Site of proposed junction with Ouse Valley Railway* (1864) (464206). From here for 1,400yd westward to Buckham Hill (452205) the never-completed formation of the latter can be traced. Some evidence of embankment, but much of this levelled. Main survival is a deep cutting along Beechen Wood, which can be approached by footpath from Buckham Hill. West of A272 at Beechen Farm (453208) there is a shallow cutting, but it is in private ground. Uckfield station (473209) present terminus of passenger service. Located west of level crossing on A22. Proposal exists for new station to the east to eliminate crossing.

EAST GRINSTEAD–CULVER JUNCTION ('THE BLUEBELL LINE') 17 miles

ACT: 10 August 1877.

OWNERSHIP: Lewes & East Grinstead Railway Co; 1878, LBSCR; 1960, Sheffield Park–Horsted Keynes leased to Bluebell Railway Co.

OPENED: 1 August 1882; re-opened to passengers with limited service, 7 August 1956; re-opened to passengers with limited service Sheffield Park–Horsted Keynes (Bluebell Halt) 1960. Bluebell Halt–Horsted Keynes, 1964.

CLOSED: Officially closed (except Horsted Keynes, for passengers), 13 June 1955 (last passenger train 28 May 1955); limited service withdrawn 17 March 1958; Horsted Keynes–East Grinstead on care and maintenance until 1960.

SETTING: The line traversed the hilly and wooded High Weald. A feature was the inconvenient sites of the stations, each of which had a very poor catchment area. The section between Sheffield Park and Horsted Keynes inclusive is operated by the Bluebell Railway. The stations have been evocatively restored. This and the magnificent collection of rolling stock makes a visit a 'must' when in the area.

REMAINS: *East Grinstead*: station* (387382) (see section Three Bridges–Groombridge Junction for full account of railway remains at East Grinstead). Imberhorne Viaduct* (383378), rails laid over it as shunting neck. The formation exists to *Kingscote station* (368355), now a private house; goods yard in use as industrial premises. Note the isolated position of the station, named after Kingscote House (372364). *West Hoathly*: site of station (371328) completely cleared and nothing left of station or goods yard. Note station 130ft below road at Sharpthorne village up steep station road and 220ft below West Hoathly Church. Sharpthorne Tunnel (730yd) at end of deep cutting south of station. *Horsted Keynes*: station and goods yard* (372293) in use by Bluebell Railway. Very well restored. Lines end 500yd to north. Note village centre 1⅛ miles to south-east. *Sheffield Park*: station and goods yard (404237) southern terminus and headquarters* of Bluebell Railway. Station splendidly restored. Station named after nearby estate and mansion. Bridge over A272 south of station removed and right-of-way much interrupted beyond. Bridge and deep cutting at Lane End Common (404222). *Newick*: cutting under A272 at 401211 completely filled-in and very hard to trace formation. The site of Newick & Chailey station and goods yard (402209) obliterated by housing development. One hundred yards east of former overbridge on A272 Lower Station Road leads south. On right 200yd down SR 'notice of private road' together with some railway fencing indicates site of station forecourt. Although environs built-up since closure, station inconvenient. Newick village centre one mile to east and Chailey (little more than a church) 1·7 miles south-west. *Barcombe*: Barcombe station (417407).* Stationmaster's house, station building, single platform all in good order. Cutting crossed by road Barcombe–

Barcombe Cross now overgrown by mature trees. Site of Culver Junction 426143 (p 180).

HORSTED KEYNES–COPYHOLD JUNCTION 3½ miles

ACT: 19 July 1880. *OWNERSHIP*: LBSCR.

OPENED: 3 September 1883; electrified, 1935.

CLOSED: Horsted Keynes–Copyhold Junction (*pass*), 28 October 1963; Horsted Keynes–Ardingly (*gds*), 28 October 1963.

SETTING: A double-track, electrified line leading from the busy Brighton line through most beautiful country to nowhere! Yet it involved heavy earthworks, a tunnel and a viaduct.

REMAINS: *Horsted Keynes*: station* (372293) in use by Bluebell Railway. Electric trains used far platform, devoid of shelter. Formation can be seen curving west from Bluebell Railway immediately south of platforms. Site of viaduct (367288), high embankment on either side. Lyewood Common (355284) 230yd tunnel with brick portals and generous loading gauge. Rather difficult to find cutting and portal to east of road through wood. Look for SR concrete posts and wire fencing. *Ardingly*: station (340276).* Whole area now railhead for aggregate traffic. Station building on roadside rehabilitated as offices. Stairs down to platform. Overbridge to east on road from Ardingly to Lindfield, past the school. Note isolation of station, only inn and four cottages near, village 1¼ miles to north. Single line to Copyhold Junction, which can be seen from overbridge at 327266. The remains of the uncompleted Ouse Valley Railway of 1864 can be seen from Copyhold Lane, 700yd east of bridge. These consist of wooded embankment on either side of road.

KEMP TOWN 1¼ miles

ACT: 13 May 1864. *OWNERSHIP*: LBSCR.

OPENED: 2 August 1869; re-opened (*pass*), 10 August 1919.

CLOSED: temporarily (*pass*), 1 January 1917, (*pass*), 31 December 1932, (*gds*), 14 June 1971.

SETTING: The Victorian suburbs of Brighton on the sides of the deep and steep-sided Lewes Road valley. All but half the length of the branch was in tunnel and the rest on embankment or viaduct.

REMAINS: Kemp Town Junction (317059) 200yd east of short tunnel under Ditchling Road. Signal box probably original structure. Lewes Road station site (319060). Viaduct over Lewes Road (A26) demolished (322058), ditto smaller one over Hartington Road. Site of Halt on south side 323057. Line now grass track behind Old Viaduct Court. Cutting to north portal

Kemp Town Tunnel filled in and part of playground of Elm Grove school. South portal within Freshfield Road industrial estate (on site of goods yard) and in use for storage. Kemp Town station (323024) demolished.

GROUP 5—WEST SUSSEX

THE DYKE BRANCH 3½ miles

ACT: 2 August 1877.

OWNERSHIP: Brighton & Dyke Railway; 1923, SR.

OPENED: 1 September 1877; re-opened 26 July 1920.

CLOSED: temporarily, 1 January 1917; 1 January 1939.

SETTING: A very steeply-graded and spectacular route rising 400ft up through the modern suburbs of Hove and thence through open downland with spectacular seaward views.

REMAINS: Dyke Junction (287056) west of Aldrington station. Line traceable by 'curve' of Harrington's Coach Works and Amhurst Cres to Old Shoreham Road. Footpath from Holmes Ave to Maple Gdns and thence behind Elm Drive and Rowan Ave. Site of *Rowan Halt* where path leads into the latter. Thence via alley to West Way, along Kingston Close and Poplar Close and as bank above footpath to golf clubhouse. Platform of *Golf Club Halt* extant at 266094. Footpath thence to *Dyke* station (260104) occupied by farm buildings. Approach road can be seen. Remains of funicular railway down to Poynings (258113) are visible north of Devil's Dyke.

SHOREHAM–ITCHINGFIELD JUNCTION (CHRIST'S HOSPITAL) 17 miles

ACT: 12 July 1858. *OWNERSHIP*: LBSCR.

OPENED: Shoreham–Partridge Green, 1 July 1861; Partridge Green–Itchingfield Junction, 16 September 1861.

CLOSED: Shoreham–Itchingfield Junction (*pass*), Beeding Cement Works–Itchingfield Junction (*gds*), 7 March 1966.

SETTING: Runs up wide Adur valley through gap in South Downs, across flat country and then through wooded High Weald.

REMAINS: West Sussex County Council has designated most of the line a bridleway, the 'Downs Link'. It can therefore be walked the whole way north of Steyning as footpaths allow the few obstructions to be easily by-passed.* *Shoreham*: junction with Brighton–Worthing line 440yd west of station (053218). Single track still laid to sidings at Beeding Cement Works. Line ends at site of bridge across River Adur (197086). From 191100 to 182113 line incorporated into Steyning by-pass. *Bramber Station* (186105): obliterated by roundabout.

Steyning Station (182113) demolished, though large goods warehouse remains. Retaining wall on south side of by-pass of railway engineering brick. Downs Link begins just south of Adur bridge. *Henfield Station* (206161): well west of old village, approached by Upper and Lower Station roads, overbridge on former and underbridge on latter removed. Station and goods yard between bridges occupied by a close of houses (appropriately 'Beechings'). *Partridge Green*: station (190189) site now a small housing area. Southern Railway concrete fence on right side approach road. South parapet of bridge remains but cutting on north side filled. *West Grinstead Station* (184225): isolated location. Building well preserved. Very large stationmaster's house. *Southwater Station* (157264): in use as dwelling but extremely delapidated. Platforms remain, also LBSC wood fencing on approach. Telephone exchange on site of goods yard. *Itchingfield Junction* (144283): where line joined Mid-Sussex line reached by bridleway.

CHRIST'S HOSPITAL–PEASMARSH JUNCTION (GUILDFORD) 15½ miles

ACT: 6 August 1860.

OWNERSHIP: Horsham & Guildford Direct Railway; 1864, LBSCR.

OPENED: 2 October 1865.

CLOSED: 14 June 1965 (though goods facilities previously withdrawn from all stations except Baynards).

SETTING: runs through heavily-wooded and extremely beautiful Wealden scenery with picturesque villages.

REMAINS: The line has been designated a bridleway. The West Sussex County Council has signposted its part south of Baynards Tunnel. Waverley District Council, which has care of the section north of the tunnel advises users to do so at their own risk. One can use the right-of-way if one can get along it; two of the river bridges are down. *Christ's Hospital Station* (148292): has recently been rebuilt out of all recognition, but the three Guildford platforms can still be seen from the up platform. Spur from branch towards Itchingfield Junction has been ploughed up. *Slinfold Station* (113310): now a caravan site which blocks the right-of-way. To south well-maintained 'Downs Link' path. Two LBSC houses on far side of former level crossing. Arun bridge (see p 79) (094327). Underbridge at A281 (090330) reduced to single girder. *Rudgwick Station* (086334) demolished and health centre built on site of station building. *Baynards*: * north approach to tunnel filled up with town refuse, but landscaped. Station (077351) in private hands and beautifully restored. Surrey Industrial Group award (1985). Picnic area on site of goods yard. Note isolation–at entrance to Baynards Park. 300yd to north, gate of private siding to fuller's earth plant. Siding can be traced for some way. *Cranleigh Station* (056391): note very convenient location in High Street. Site of station and goods yard occupied by shopping precinct. Rear access road along track from level crossing on Knowle Lane, railway house on other side. *Bramley*: bridge over river at 036407 restored. Site of Birtley Siding north of underbridge (018435). *Bramley Station* (010451) building demolished, builders' merchant in goods yard. Bridges at 005458 over railway and Wey Navigation. Former overbridge on A281 at Stone Bridge removed and road re-aligned, destroying site of Stone Bridge Sidings. Bridge over River Wey at 995464 removed. *Peasmarsh Junction* (992469): with Portsmouth Direct line. Uncompleted curve, completely overgrown with large trees, can be seen curving east to Redhill line at 997471.

WEST SUSSEX RAILWAY: CHICHESTER–SELSEY 8¼ miles

ACT: 29 April 1896, Chichester–Selsey; West Sussex (Selsey Tramway Section) Railway Certificate, 1924 (*sic*), Selsey Beach Extension.

OWNERSHIP: Hundred of Manhood & Selsey Tramway.

OPENED: Chichester–Selsey 27 August 1897; Selsey Beach 1 August 1898.

CLOSED: Selsey Beach Extension fell out of use about 1906; Chichester–Selsey, 19 January 1935.

SETTING: From Chichester across the flat low-lying peninsula of Selsey Bill through farmland and new housing estates.

REMAINS: It must be remembered the line had few earthworks and bridges and a few shacks. In the forty years since closure great changes have occurred, and tracing the line is difficult. *Chichester*: site of station between back gardens of houses in Terminus Road, and BR station now occupied by sidings (858042). Curved row of trees on edge of school playing field represents line. Footpath* opposite Post Office in Stockbridge Road (487036) is along line, and this can be followed along canal bank to site of bridge across it (860020). Note new inn, 'The Selsey Tram' at corner Stockbridge Road and St George's Drive, 'freelance' locomotive has replaced Shefflex railcar on sign. *Hunston*: right-of-way a path from canal (bridge removed) to site of level crossing over B2145 at bus shelter (015859);* station was on east side. Hoe Farm private halt

(863003). *Sidlesham*: site of *Chalder Station* (860992) on Chalder Lane west side of Chalder Farm Cottages. Site of Millpond Halt on north side Rookery Lane behind cottage on corner with B2145. South of lane, line of bushes represents right-of-way. *Sidlesham Station* (860972) on north side of Mill Lane. Right-of-way footpath* along Tramway Bank across end of Pagham Harbour. *Selsey*: site of Ferry Siding Halt at south end of Tramway Bank at level crossing across B2145. Right-of-way can be traced (but not walked) to site of Golf Club Halt (855944) on north side of Golf Links Lane at junction with drive up to club house. No trace of *Selsey Bridge Halt* where line crossed under B2145. *Selsey Station* (860937): site just north of Stargazers Hotel under junction of Manor and Beach Roads, through two small triangular open spaces survive. No trace of extension, but roughly along line of Beach Road.

CHICHESTER–MIDHURST 11$\frac{7}{8}$ miles

ACT: 39–40 Vic. c.109, 1876, (reviving lapsed powers).

OWNERSHIP: LBSCR.

OPENED: 11 July 1881.

CLOSED: (*pass*) 6 July 1935; Lavant–Midhurst (*gds*) 1953; Snakes Lane–Lavant (*gds*) 1972.

SETTING: Across the coastal plain and with heavy grades across the South Downs. Because of the heavy earthworks line can be easily traced, but cannot be walked as it is very overgrown or in private ownership.

REMAINS: *Chichester*: station (858042) rebuilt by BR when it still believed in architecture. Fishbourne crossing over A259 the junction between Brighton–Worthing line and branch. Line extant to gravel pits at overbridge on Snakes Lane (855077). *Lavant Station** (855086): in deep cutting, station building at top. Like the other two, very large two-storey, brick below and half-timber above. North to overbridge on A286 (156121) line visible on valley floor. North of overbridge heavy earthworks on valley side west of road. Westdean Tunnel 417yd. *Singleton Station** (867130): substantial station building at end of tree-lined approach. Now shop for Chilsdown Vineyard. Retaining wall of large station. Drove Tunnel 717yd. Cocking Tunnel 700yd. *Cocking Station** (875176): at underbridge on Bell Lane, now private house, goods yard now well-kept garden. Can be seen from other side of line from farm lane. At Cocking Causeway line now a pig farm. Line at *Midhurst* described in next section.

HARDHAM JUNCTION (PULBOROUGH)–PETERSFIELD 19¾ miles

ACT: 10 August 1857, Hardham Junction–Petworth; 13 August 1859, Petworth–Midhurst; 23 July 1860, Midhurst–Petersfield.

OWNERSHIP: Mid-Sussex Railway (Hardham Junction–Petworth): 1864 LBSCR. Midhurst & Mid-Sussex Junction (Petworth–Midhurst); 1874 LBSCR. Petersfield Railway (Midhurst –Petersfield): 1863 L&SWR.

OPENED: Hardham Junction–Petworth, 10 October 1859; Petworth–Midhurst, 15 October 1866; Midhurst–Petersfield, 1 September 1864; Midhurst, LBSCR–Midhurst LSWR (*gds*) 17 December 1866, (*pass*) 12 July 1925.

CLOSED: Hardham Junction–Petersfield (*pass*), Midhurst–Petersfield (*gds*) 5 February 1955; Midhurst–Petworth (*gds*) 12 October 1864; Petworth–Hardham Junction (*gds*) 23 May 1966.

SETTING: Ran through very beautiful countryside up the well-wooded Rother valley (the West Sussex one!) with the South Downs to the south and the High Weald to the north. Midhurst is a delightful old town, as are many of the villages.

REMAINS: The line can easily be traced, but cannot be walked for any distance. *Pulborough Station* (043187): on Mid-Sussex line, the starting point of branch trains, though up loop platform is now out of use. *Hardham Junction* (035175): site south-west of level crossing on lane to Hardham Mill from A29. *Fittleworth Station* (008181): at overbridge on B2138. Pair of stucco LBSCR cottages, but station demolished. Cuttings filled with a veritable jungle. *Petworth Station** (970192): at over-bridge on A285 near Coultershaw Mill 1¾ miles south of town centre. Wooden building tastefully restored as dwelling. Two well restored pairs of railway cottages. Shop in former goods warehouse. *Selham Station* (933205): on high embankment west of road (underbridge removed). Wood building now private house and cannot be approached. *Midhurst**: tunnel (290yd) —east portal still open, west portal bricked up. *1881 LBSCR station* (884207), site has been completely built over. Entrance to estate is by former station approach off New Road (B2226), houses and maisonettes along The Fairway built along the line up to tunnel. Lower part of estate built across site of junction with Chichester line. Embankment parallel with New Road removed. Bepton Road underbridge (879211) removed. Original LBSCR station to east, goods yard now timber yard (note goods shed). LSWR station to west on slightly higher level than through line. Very much modified and occupied by consulting engineers. Industrial estate on

LSW yard. Two LSWR cottages in good condition. *Elsted Station* (834206): note isolation (except for 'Railway Inn'). Goods yard now tractor depot, new office/flat on site of station building on platform. *Rogate Station* (805219): in Nyewood hamlet. Plain stucco station building now plastics factory. *Petersfield*: underbridge across A3 (750237) and approach embankments removed. Station (744236) on Portsmouth Direct line, large gothic style range of buildings. Site of Midhurst bay on down side north of level crossing. Note second arch for branch on overbridge to north.

HAVANT–HAYLING ISLAND $4\frac{1}{2}$ miles

ACT: 23 July 1860; 12 August 1867 (diversion to shore route).

OWNERSHIP: Hayling Railways; 1923 LBSCR.

OPENED: Havant–Langston (*gds*) 1 January 1865: Havant–Hayling (*pass*), Langston–Hayling (*gds*) 8 July 1867.

CLOSED: 4 November 1963.

SETTING: Ran through the rapidly-growing town of Havant, across Langstone Channel and along west shore of low-lying Hayling Island (highest point 22ft above sea level), now rapidly becoming submerged under bungalows and caravans.

REMAINS: *Havant*: station (718067) rebuilt 1938 with central through roads, Hayling bay on down platform, now bus park. Fairfield Road level crossing—branch crossed road just south of signal box. Line can be walked through town as far as Langstone. Overbridge on Havant by-pass (721057). *Langstone*: * no trace of Langston station (note railway spelling) or of level crossing (717050) due to widening and relocation of A3023 opposite Langstone High Street. Embankment and foundations opening bridge across Langstone Channel (718043). On island, line walkable (unofficially) most of the way on embankment along shore. It is a great pity that the local authority does not appear to be making this into a pedestrian way. *North Hayling*: site of halt at end of short lane to shore opposite Victoria Road (718030). *South Hayling:* site of Hayling Island Station (710998) on north side Station Road, buildings gone; platforms and goods shed remain. Near St Mary's church, South Hayling, 'Hayling Billy' pub.

GROUP 6—STONE BLOCKS AND IRON RAILS

SURREY IRON RAILWAY $9\frac{1}{2}$ miles

CROYDON MERSTHAM & GODSTONE RAILWAY $8\frac{1}{2}$ miles

WANDSWORTH–MERSTHAM

ACT: 21 May 1801 (41 Geo III c.33) (SIR); 17 May 1803 (43

Geo III c.35) (CM&G).

OWNERSHIP: Surrey Iron Railway (Wandsworth–Pitlake, Croydon); Croydon Merstham & Godstone Railway (Pitlake–Greystone Lime Quarry, Merstham); 1838, LBSCR compelled to purchase CM&G; 1846, LBSCR; 1844, SIR purchased by LSWR; 1846, part of right-of-way sold to LBSCR.

OPENED: Wandsworth–Pitlake (*gds*) 26 July 1803; Hackbridge branch (*gds*), June 1804; Pitlake–Merstham (*gds*), July 1805.

CLOSED: Pitlake–Merstham, date uncertain but track lifted in 1838; Wandsworth–Pitlake, 31 August 1846.

GAUGE: 4ft 6in between centres of holes in stone blocks.

SETTING: These were the only pre-locomotive railways in south-east England; the SIR was the first public railway in the whole country.

REMAINS: *Wandsworth*: terminus was former basin (256752) between River Wandle–Armoury Way–Fairfield St. From here south along York Road then Garrett Lane at intervals to Summerstown. (Later, LSWR crossed SIR at Earlsfield.) Crossed Plough Lane and ran close to Mead Path (along west side Lambeth Cemetery). Through Wandle Park to Cross *Merton High Street* (A24) at *Colliers Wood LTE Station* (268704). Along Church Road to where latter curves sharply east. Along Ravensbury Park and through sports ground to cross London Road (A216) at *Mitcham Station* (273681). From here the Wimbledon–West Croydon railway substantially follows the original line through *Mitcham Jct Station* (284677), *Beddington Lane Station* (293672) to *Waddon Marsh Station* (309661). Beyond, course lost under gas-works. *Croydon*: the terminus was at Pitlake (317656), where Waddon New Road and railway run alongside each other (note 'Pitlake Arms'). Site marked by 132 Waddon New Road*. *Connection between Pitlake and Croydon Canal Basin*: owned by Croydon Canal Co. From Pitlake along line of Tamworth Road to basin (now occupied by West Croydon station, 323661). The CM&G formed an end-on junction with the SIR at Pitlake. Though no trace remains through central Croydon the line was roughly along line of Church Street–north of Church–Church Road (formerly Tramway Road). Continuous passage behind houses east side of Southbridge. Crossed road at north junction with Dering Road. Along Barham Road (off Warham Road). Across Hayling Park in front of Whitgift School (324640). At Avon Road, a right-of-way (Avon Path) leads north and south as two cul-de-sacs, which are the course of the line. Line passed just east of *St Augustine's Church*. Line passed just in front of Hayling Chalk Pit (321625), where houses in Biddulph Road are on site of lime kilns. Property boundaries on 6in map show line of railway. To south line represented by right-of-way behind houses along A253. At *Rotary Field** recreation ground (326621), a narrow terrace on hillside remains, and on this a short length of track has been restored. The line now diverged west from Brighton Road. Gardens in Foxley Lane show evidence of terracing. A23 and Banstead Road (B280) crossed line at junction with Foxley Lane (311617). Line now converges with Brighton Road (A23). Purley Rise and Downlands along line, thence along The Drive (terracing in gardens). *Coulsdon*: line crossed Chipstead Valley Road (B2032) by bridge approached by curved embankments (296596). No trace of bridge or embankments, but site marked by Elim chapel. On south side line ran through grounds of Cane Hill Hospital, but obliterated by LBSCR Quarry Line (298589). Line crossed A23 on level at junction with Hollyme Oak Road and Wood Place Lane (293581). Faint traces of terracing can be seen in field behind telephone exchange in Hollyme Oak Road. South of 'Star Inn', *Hooley* (288568), houses on east side of A23 built on spoil heaps from cuttings. North portal of Merstham Tunnel 70yd north of Dean Lane (east from A23) (289558). On north side of Dean Lane is brick parapet and abutments of overbridge* over the line, which ran through site of the café. Line of track can be seen in gardens of houses on east side A23 as far as lane to Dean Lane Farm. 20yd up lane, brick parapet of bridge over line on north side of lane*. New roundabout, motorway overbridge and motorway access road have destroyed traces of line. Opposite Harper's Oak Lane (west from A23) (287545) just on east side of main road is a deep overgrown cutting*. Line swung east from road behind 'Jolliffe Arms' (W. J. Jolliffe a promoter of the CM&G). The length of track preserved south of inn, not on line of railway. Note Weybridge Cottage north of inn (288544), built by Banks in 1805, also former stables.

Index

Numbers in bold indicate a reference in the Gazetteer

Allhallows-on-sea, 88, 91–3, **167–8**
Appledore, 97–100, **170**
Ardingly, 52, 60, 65, 68, 76, **182**
Ash (Kent), 38, **156**

Barcombe, 59, 63, **181**; —Mills, 59, 66, 68–9, **180**
Barham, 116–17, **154**, **160**
Baynards, 79–81, 83, **184**
Bexhill-on-sea, 101–2, **175**
Biddenden, 42–4, **173**
Bishopsbourne, 117, **160**
Bluebell Rly, 58–9, 63–4, 68, 73, **180–1**
Bodiam, 41, 43, 45–6, **172**
Bramber, 76, **183**
Bramley, 79–80, **185**
Brasted, 140, **175**
Bridge, 117, **160**
Brighton, 10, 12, 14–15, 46, 49, 50–8, 60–4, 69, 74–8, 88, 101, 105, 141–6, **182–3**; —& the Dyke Rly, 141–2, **183**

Chatham, 13, 111, 114, 119–21, **164**
Camber —Sands, 146–7, **171**
Canterbury, 13, 37–8, 106, 111, 116–18, 132–5, **160–1**; —& Whitstable Rly, 132–5, **160–1**; -Rd, 39, **156**
Chattenden & Upnor Lt Rly, 147–8, **164–5**; —Naval Tramway, 148–9, **165–6**
Croydon, 27, 50, 55–6, 58, 62, 66; —Merstham & Godstone Rly, 150–2, **188–90**
Cuckoo Line, 10, 56, 60–5, 70, **178–9**

Dover Harbour, 136–7; —& Martin Mill Lt Rly, 137, **158–9**
Dungeness, 97–101, 123, **170**
Dunton Green, 140, **175**
Dyke, the Devil's, 141–2, **183**

Eastchurch, 93–5, **163**
East Grinstead, 51, 56–67, 73, **176**, **181**; ——Groombridge & Tunbridge Wells Rly, 52, **176**; ——Rly, 52, **176**
East Kent (Lt) Rlys, 33–40, 132, **155–6**
Eastry, 38–9, **155**

Elham, 115–18, **160**; —Valley Lt Rly, 115–16, **159–60**
Elsted, 85, **188**
Elvington, 38, **155**
Eridge, 56, 61–3, 70, 73, **178**
Eythorne, 38–9, **155**

Faversham and —Quay, 12, 13, 111, 119, 131–2, **161–2**
Fawkham, 127–8, **168**
Fittleworth, 85, **187**
Folkestone, 12, 88, 96, 99, 115–16, 118, 122, 132, **159**
Forest Row, 59, 60, 70, 76, **177**
Frittenden Rd, 42, 44, **173**

Goudhurst, 20–2, 24, 28, 30, **174**
Grain, 122, 131, **167**
Grange Rd, 66, **176**
Gravesend, 123, 124–9, **168**; —Rly, 123, 127, **167–8**
Greatstone-on-sea, 99, **170**
Groombridge, 52, 55, 60–7, 73, **177**

Hailsham, 52, 55–6, 62, 65, 70, **179**
Hamsey, 69–70, **179**
Hartfield, 67, **177**
Havant, 8, 74, 102–3, **188**
Hawkhurst, 15–16, 19–30, 40–2, **174**
Hayling Island, 47, 88, 102–4, 138, **188**; —Rlys, 103, **188**
Headcorn, 41–5, **173**
Heathfield, 56, 62, 70, **178**
Hellingly, 59, 70, **179**
Henfield, 77, **184**
Herne Bay and Hampton Pier, 88, 132
High Halden Rd, 42, **173**
Horsham, 70, **179**
Horsmonden, 22–4, 29, 30, **174**
Horsham & Guildford Direct Rly, 78–83, **184–5**
Horsted Keynes, 57, 60–1, 63–8, **182**
Hundred of Hoo, 91, 93, 122, 129, 131, 148, **166–7**
Hundred of Manhood & Selsey Tramway, *see* West Sussex Rly

Hythe, 96–7, **169**

Isfield, 66, 69, 73, **180**

Kent & East Sussex Lt Rly, 33, 40–6, 138, **172–3**
Kingscote, 67, **181**
Kingsnorth Lt Rly, 149, **165–6**
Knowlton, 38, **155**

Langston, 102–3, **188**
Lavant, 86, **186**
Lewes, 50–1, 55, 57, 60–1, 65, 67–9, 73, 142, **180**; —& E Grinstead Rly, 56–7, 61, 66, **180–1**; —& Uckfield Rly, 51, **179**

Margate, 13, 88, 109, 111–15, **158**
Martin Mill, 137, **159**
Mayfield, 70, **178**
Midhurst, 83–7, **187–8**
Mid-Sussex Rly, 83–4, **187**; —& Midhurst Jct Rly, 84, **187**
Minster-on-Sea, 94–5, **162**

New Romney and Littlestone, 97–101, 123, **170–1**
Newick dnd Chailey, 59, 63, 68, **154**, **181**
Northiam, 41–3, **173**

Ouse Valley Rly, 52, 55, 69, **180**, **182**

Paddock Wood, 13, 19–23, 25–9, **174**
Partridge Green, 76–7, **184**
Petersfield, 8, 83–4, 86–7, **188**
Petworth, 75, 83–5, 87, **187**
Polegate, 52, 55, 64, 74, **179**
Portsmouth Direct Rly, 8, 75, 78, 80, 84, **185**
Port Victoria, 91–2, 129–31, **167**
Pulborough, 12, 83, 85–7, **187**
Purley, 152, 189

Queenborough and —Pier, 93–5, 129–31, **162–3**

Ramsgate, 13, 15, 29, 88, 111–15, 129, **158**
Richborough, 37, 39, 122, 132, **156**
Rochester, 119–21, 131, **164**
Robertsbridge, 40–1, 43–5, **172**
Rogate, 85, **188**
Rolvenden, 41–6, **173**
Rosherville, 127–8, **168**
Rotherfield, 64, 70, **178**
Rother Valley Lt Rly, 40, 45, **172–3**
Rowfant, 65–6, **176**
Rudgwick, 79–80, **184**
Rye and— Rye Harbour, 24, 97, 136–7, 146–7, **171**; —& Camber Tramway, 33, 138, 146–7, **171**

Salehurst, 41, **172**
Sandgate, 96–7, **169**
Sandling, 96–7, **169**
Sandwich, 38–9, **156**
Selham, 85, **187**
Selsey, 47–8, 88, **186**
Sharnal Street, 129, 148–9, **166–7**
Sheerness, 93–4, 129; —East, 94, **162**
Sheffield Park, 52, 59, 60, 62–3, 68, **181**
Shepherd's Well, 37, 39, **155**
Sheppey, Isle of, 93, **162–3**; —Lt Rly, 33, 93–5, **162–3**
Shoreham (Sussex), 75–7, 81, 122, 138, **183**
Sidlesham, 47, **186**
Sidley, 101, **175**
Singleton, 86, **186**
Slinfold, 79, **184**
Southfleet, 128, **168**
South Street, 135, **154**, **161**
Staple, 38, **156**
Stephens, Lt-Col H. F., 15, 22, 32–3, 93, 95, 146
Steyning, 76–7, **184**
Stoke (Hundred of Hoo), 91, 129, **167**
Strood, 27, 118–19, **163–4**
Surrey & Sussex Jct Rly, 55–6
Surrey Iron Rly, 150–2, **188–90**

Tenterden, 19, 40–5, **173**; —Rly, 46
Thanet, Isle of, 111–15, **157–8**
Three Bridges, 51, 60, 63–6, 75, 83, **176**
Toomer Loop, 118–19, 121, **165**

Uckfield, 51–2, 55–66, 69, 73, **180**
Upnor, 147–8, **165**

Wandsworth, 150–1, **188**
Waldron & Horeham Rd, 59, 70
Westerham, 139–40, 142, **176**; —Valley Rly, 139–41, **175**
West Grinstead, 77, **184**
West Hoathly, 59, 63, 67, **181**
West Sussex Rly, 33, 46–8, **185–6**
Whitstable, 134–6, **161**
Wingham, 37–9, **156**
Withyham, 67, **177**
Wittersham Rd, 42–3, **173**
Woodnesborough, 38, **156**